STORYFUN

2

TEACHER'S BOOK

Second edition

Karen Saxby
Lucy Frino

Cambridge University Press

www.cambridge.org/elt

Cambridge Assessment English

www.cambridgeenglish.org

Information on this title: www.cambridge.org/9781316617090

© Cambridge University Press 2017

First published 2011
Second edition 2017

20 19 18 17 16 15 14 13 12 11 10

Printed in Great Britain by CPI Group (UK) Ltd, Croydon CRO 4YY

A catalogue record for this publication is available from the British Library

ISBN 978-1-316-61702-1 Student's Book
ISBN 978-1-316-61709-0 Teacher's Book with Audio
ISBN 978-1-316-61713-7 Presentation plus

Contents

⭐ = Value		🔊 = Let's say! pages	
♪ = Song		▶ = Audio	
✔ = Test tasks for Starters		IA = Interactive activity	
➡ = Practice for Starters		🏠 = Home FUN booklet	
❋ = Let's have fun! pages		👆 = Online activities	
💬 = Let's speak! pages			

Introduction

Welcome to *Storyfun*!

Storyfun is a series of six books written for young learners aged between 6 and 12 years. The series provides story-based preparation for the Cambridge English: Young Learners tests (YLE). Each Student's Book contains eight stories with activities that include vocabulary and grammar tasks, puzzles, games, poems, songs and an exploration of the story 'value' (for example, an appreciation of nature, the importance of friendship). The Teacher's Books provide detailed suggestions on how to approach the storytelling, together with clear instructions for guiding learners through the unit. With a variety of flexible resources, each unit in *Storyfun* is designed to provide approximately three to four hours of class time.

Why stories?

Storyfun aims to provide an opportunity for language practice by engaging learners' interest in stories.

Research has shown that meaningful and imaginative stories can motivate learning because learners:

o   engage with the text and their imaginations.
o   learn vocabulary with repetition of key words in the text and pictures.
o   are exposed to repeated rhyme and sound patterns and accurate pronunciation.
o   develop deeper social understanding by relating to characters and events in the story.
o   actively engage listening skills as they predict, hypothesise and await outcomes.

Points to remember for effective learning:

o   Story-reading should be interactive (teacher and learners). It should involve pointing, describing and discussing how the story relates to the real world.
o   Learners will engage with a story more if they are encouraged to 'work out' the meaning, for example, why learners think characters did something or how characters felt at a certain moment and, of course, what the story 'value' is.
o   Learners benefit from more than one reading or hearing of a story. At least one reading should be read/heard right the way through from beginning to end without interruption.

For more information about stories in language learning, go to

Why Cambridge English: Young Learners (YLE)?

The stories have been written to reflect the different language levels and topic areas of the Cambridge English: Starters, Movers and Flyers tests and to appeal to the target-reader age groups. The language of the stories is exploited in activities that check comprehension, teach key vocabulary and grammar, practise all four language skills (reading, writing, listening and speaking) and give learners an opportunity to familiarise themselves with the nature and format of the Cambridge English: Young Learners tests. The optional *Let's have fun!* and *Let's speak!* sections at the back of the books also provide opportunities for collaborative learning and test speaking practice. The *Let's say!* pages support early pronunciation skills, building from sounds to sentences.

There are two Student's Books for each test: pre-A1 (Starters), A1 (Movers) and A2 (Flyers). *Storyfun 1* gently introduces students to the Cambridge English: Starters language and topics through fun activities and test-style practice. Activities are carefully graded to ensure learners are guided towards the test level, with frequent opportunities to build up their language and skills. *Storyfun 2* provides examples of all the Cambridge English: Starters test tasks. By the end of Storyfun levels 1 and 2, constant recycling of language and test task types ensures learners are fully prepared for the Cambridge English: Starters test.

Who is *Storyfun* for?

Storyfun has been written for teachers and young learners of English in a wide variety of situations. It is suitable for:

o   learners in this age group who enjoy reading and listening to stories
o   large and small groups of learners
o   monolingual and multilingual classes
o   learners who are beginning preparation for the Cambridge English: Starters test
o   young learners who need to develop their vocabulary, grammar and language
o   young learners keen to discuss social values, develop collaborative learning skills and build confidence for the Starters Speaking paper
o   teachers who wish to develop their learners' literacy skills

What are the key features of *Storyfun 2*?

Student's Book

o   eight imaginative and motivating stories
o   fun, interactive, creative and meaningful activities
o   activities similar to task types found in all three parts (Reading and Writing, Listening and Speaking) of the Cambridge English: Starters test

- an introduction to Cambridge English: Starters grammar and vocabulary
- extension activities *Let's have fun!*, further speaking practice *Let's speak!* and an early pronunciation focus *Let's say!*
- a unit-by-unit word list

Home FUN booklet

- fun activities for learners to try at home
- 'self-assessment' activities that build learners' confidence and encourage autonomy
- a Cambridge English: Starters picture dictionary
- *Let's have fun!* pages to encourage learners to use English in the wider world
- answers, audio and additional support found online by using the access code at the front of the book.

Teacher's Book with Audio

- a map of the Student's Book (topics, grammar points and Starters test practice for each unit)
- practical step-by-step notes with suggestions for:

  - ✓ personalisation at presentation and practice stages
  - ✓ skills work: reading, writing, listening, speaking, drawing and colouring
  - ✓ pair and group work
  - ✓ puzzles, games, poems and songs
  - ✓ speaking activities and projects
  - ✓ discussion tasks to explore the story 'value'
  - ✓ recycling of language
  - ✓ incorporating digital materials into the lesson

- Cambridge English: Starters test tips
- full audioscripts
- imaginative audio recordings for stories and activities (downloadable by using the access code at the front of this book) reflective of the Cambridge English: Starters Listening test.
- photocopiable pages for the Student's Book or optional extension activities
- links to online practice and the Home FUN booklet

Presentation plus

- digital version of all Student's Book pages
- interactive Student's Book activities
- audio played directly from the digital page
- digital flashcards with audio
- digital slideshow of every story
- an Image carousel that provides further visuals associated with story themes
- integrated tools to make notes and highlight activities

Online practice

For the teacher
- Presentation plus
- All audio recordings
- Additional digital resources to support your classes

For the Student
- Fun activities to practise the exam, skills and language
- All audio recordings
- Additional digital resources

Word FUN World app

- Cambridge English: Young Learners vocabulary game
- For mobile phones and tablets

Storytelling

Why should we use stories in language learning classes?

There are several reasons! A good story encourages us to turn the next page and read more. We want to find out what happens next and what the main characters do and say to each other. We may feel excited, sad, afraid, angry or really happy. The experience of reading or listening to a story is likely to make us 'feel' that we are part of the story, too. Just like in our 'real' lives, we might love or hate different characters. Perhaps we recognise ourselves or other people we know in some of the story characters. Perhaps they have similar talents, ambitions, weaknesses or problems. Because of this natural connection with story characters, our brains process the reading of stories differently from the way we read factual information. This is because our brains don't always recognise the difference between an imagined situation and a real one so the characters become 'alive' to us. What they say or do is therefore <u>much more meaningful</u>. The words and structures that relate a story's events, descriptions and conversations are processed by learners in a deeper way.

Encouraging learners to read or listen to stories should therefore help them to learn a second language in a way that is not only fun, but memorable.

How else do stories help?

Stories don't only offer the young reader a chance to learn more vocabulary and develop their grammatical skills. The experience also creates an opportunity to develop critical and creative thinking, emotional literacy and social skills. As learners read a story, they will be imagining far more details than its words communicate. Each learner will, subconsciously, be 'animating' the characters and making judgements and predictions about events.

As a teacher, you can encourage creativity and critical thinking by asking learners in groups to develop characters in more detail, talk about the part of the story they enjoyed most/least or even write different endings. You can also discuss, in English or L1 if necessary, the story 'values'; in other words, what different stories teach us about how to relate to others.

Stories also offer a forum for personalised learning. No two learners will feel exactly the same about a story and an acceptance of difference can also be interesting to explore and discuss in class.

How can we encourage learners to join in and ask parents to help?

If, at first, learners lack confidence or motivation to read stories in English, help by reading the story to them without stopping so learners are just enjoying the story, stress free, and following as well as they can by looking at the pictures. During a second reading you might encourage interaction by asking questions like *Is this funny, scary or sad?* (Starters) *Was that a good idea?* (Movers) *What do you think will happen next?* (Flyers). If the class is read to in a relaxed and fun way, learners will subconsciously relate to the reading and language learning process more confidently and positively. Of course, being read to by a parent at home, too, is also simply a lovely way to share quiet and close time. To engage parents in the language learning process, you might share some

of the above points with them or encourage them to search online for language learning activities to do at home with their children.

The Home FUN booklet has been specially designed for learners to use at home with parents. Activities are fun and easy to follow, requiring little instruction. The booklet aims to help learners show parents what they have learnt at school and to engage them in the learning process.

Further suggestions for storytelling

o   Involve learners in the topic and ask guessing and prediction questions in L1 if necessary. This will engage learners in the process of storytelling and motivate learning. When you pause the audio during the story, ask learners:

➢   about the topic and themselves

➢   to guess aspects of the story

➢   to say how they think a character feels or what they may say next

o   If you are telling the story yourself, support your learners in any way you can by adding your own dramatisation. For instance, you can read the stories with as much animation as possible and use props such as puppets or soft toys and different voices to bring the stories to life.

o   Incorporate the use of realia into the storytelling process. For example, if you are using *Storyfun 1*, in 'Kim's birthday' you could set up the classroom to look like a party with balloons, cards and presents, and in 'Let's go there now' you could bring different sports equipment into the classroom to use.

o   Once learners are familiar with the story they could even act out parts of the story in role plays. This will not only involve learners in the stories and add a fun element but can also help in practising and consolidating language.

Suggestions for using the story pictures

For skills practice

o   Before listening to the story, learners look at all the pictures on the story pages and discuss in small groups who or what they think the story is about and what are the key events.

o   Learners trace a picture (adding their own choice of extra details) and then follow your colouring or drawing instructions.

To encourage creative thinking

o   Groups choose two people in a picture and imagine what they are saying to each other. They then write a question with answer or a short dialogue.

o   Groups choose a background person in a picture and invent details about him/her. For example, how old they are, what they like doing, where they live, what pet they have.

o   Groups invent details that are unseen in the picture, for example, ten things in a bag, cupboard or garden.

o   Learners imagine they are 'in' the picture. What is behind / in front of / next to them? What can they feel (the sun, a cold wind …), smell (flowers, cooking …) or hear (birds, traffic …)?

To revise vocabulary and grammar

o Learners find as many things in a picture as they can which begin with a particular letter, for example, 'f'.

o Learners list things in a picture that are a certain colour or place. For example, what someone is wearing or what is on the table.

o Learners choose four things they can see in a picture and list the words according to the size of the object or length of the word. Learners could also choose things according to categories such as food or animals.

o Use the pictures to revise grammar, for example *This is / These are*.

o Choose a picture in the story and ask learners in groups to say what is happening in this part of the story.

o Practise prepositions by asking learners what they can see in a picture in different places, for example, in the box, on the table or under the tree.

o Practise question forms by asking learners about different aspects of a picture, for example: *What colour is the cat? How many ducks are there? What's the boy doing?*

o On the board, write the first and last letter of four things learners can remember in a particular story picture. Learners complete the words.

o Point to objects or people in a picture and ask *This/These yes/no* questions. For example: *Is this a shoe? Are these toys? Is this a boy? Are these hats?*

o Ask *yes/no* colour and *how many* questions. For example, point to an apple and ask *Is this apple blue? Can you see four apples?*

o Show learners a story picture for 30 seconds and then ask *What's in that picture?* Write learners' answers on the board.

o Ask simple *What's the word* questions and build on known vocabulary sets. For example: *It's green. You can eat it. It's a fruit.* (a pear / an apple / a grape / a kiwi)

Suggestions for using the word list

At the back of the Student's Book, learners will find a list of important Starters words that appear in each unit.

o Play 'Which word am I?' Learners work in pairs, looking at the word list for the unit. Choose a noun and give the class clues about it until one pair guesses it. Don't make the clues too easy and focus on form first and meaning afterwards. Say, for example: *I've got four letters. The letter 'k' is in me. You can sit on me. You can ride me to school.* (bike)

o Divide the class into A and B pairs. Learner A sits facing the board. Learner B sits with his/her back to the board. Write four words (nouns or verbs are best) from the word list for the unit on the board. Learner A then draws or mimes them until their partner guesses them all and writes them correctly (with the help of Learner A who can only say *Yes, that's right!* or *No, that's wrong!*). When everyone has finished, learners change places. Write some new words on the board. Learner B in each pair mimes these words for Learner A to guess.

o Play 'Tell me more, please!' Choose a noun from the word list for the unit and write it on the board, for example: *banana*. Learners take turns to add more information about the banana. For example, Learner A says: *The banana is long.* Learner B adds: *The banana is long. It's yellow.* Learner C says: *The banana is long. It's yellow. It's a fruit.* Continue until learners can't remember previous information.

o Pairs work together to make as many words from the word list for the unit as they can, using a number of letters that you dictate to the class. Alternatively, use word tiles from board games or letter cards made by the class. These could also be used for spelling tests in pairs or groups.

o On the board, write eight words from the word list for the unit with the letters jumbled. Pairs work as fast as they can to find the words and spell them correctly.

o On the board, write eight words from the word list for the unit. Spell three or four of them incorrectly. Pairs work as fast as they can to identify the misspelt words (they shouldn't be told how many there are) and to write them down correctly.

o Play 'Make a word'. Each group chooses a word (four, five or six letters long) from the word list for the unit and creates it by forming a human sculpture, i.e. learners in each group stand in a line, using their arms or legs to create the shapes of each letter. Remember you may need two learners for some letters (e.g. 'k'). When all the groups are ready, the words are guessed.

o Use the word list for the unit to play common word games such as hangman, bingo and definition games or for dictated spelling tests. A common alternative to the traditional hangman, which learners may enjoy, is an animal with its mouth open, with 8–10 steps leading down into its mouth. (You could use a crocodile at Starters, a shark at Movers or a dinosaur at Flyers.) With each incorrect guess, the stick person falls down onto the next step, and gets eaten if they reach the animal's mouth!

For more information on Cambridge English: Young Learners, please visit. From here, you can download the handbook for teachers, which includes information about each level of the Young Learners tests. You can also find information for candidates and their parents, including links to videos of the Speaking test at each level. There are also sample test papers, as well as further games and songs and links to the Teaching Support website.

A few final classroom points

Please try to be as encouraging as possible when working through the activities. By using phrases such as *Now you! You choose! Well done! Don't worry!* (all on the Starters word list) you are also helping learners to feel more confident about participating fully in the class and trying hard to do their best. Make sure that everyone in your class adds to open class work, however minimally, and when mistakes are made, view them as opportunities for learning. Try not to interrupt to correct learners during open class discussion, role plays, etc. Doing so might negatively affect a child's willingness to contribute in future. It takes courage to speak out in class. Make mental notes of mistakes and then cover them at a later moment with the whole class.

Have fun!

But most of all, please remember that an hour's lesson can feel very much longer than that to a learner who feels excluded, fearful of making mistakes, unsure about what to do, unable to follow instructions or express any personal opinions. An hour's lesson will feel like five minutes if a learner is having fun, sensing their own progress and participating fully in enjoyable and meaningful activities.

How is the Student's Book organised?

Story

Four illustrated story pages using language (topics, vocabulary and grammar) needed for the Cambridge English: Starters test.

Vocabulary activity

Each unit of four-page activities opens with a vocabulary comprehension activity related to the key Cambridge English: Starters vocabulary presented in the story.

Value key phrase

A key English phrase in a speech bubble (sometimes in bold) within the story demonstrates the story 'value'. For example, Trying your best ➜ "Can I try again?"

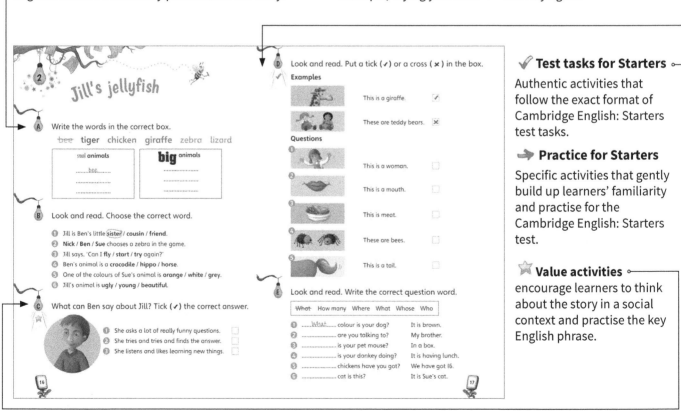

✔️ Test tasks for Starters

Authentic activities that follow the exact format of Cambridge English: Starters test tasks.

➡️ Practice for Starters

Specific activities that gently build up learners' familiarity and practise for the Cambridge English: Starters test.

☆ Value activities

encourage learners to think about the story in a social context and practise the key English phrase.

Skills

All activities develop reading, writing, listening and speaking skills useful for the YL tests.

 Songs

Open activities such as poems and songs maintain learners' motivation and interest.

 Let's have fun!

Optional projects or games at the back of the Student's Book promote collaborative learning.

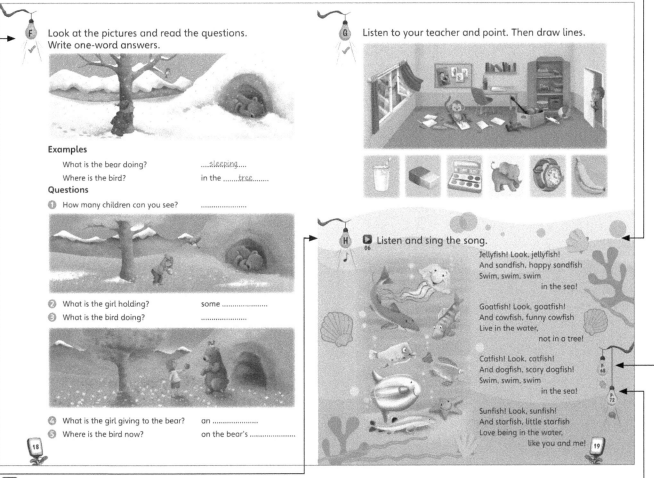

F Look at the pictures and read the questions. Write one-word answers.

Examples

What is the bear doing? ....sleeping....

Where is the bird? in the ....tree.......

Questions

1. How many children can you see? ....

2. What is the girl holding? some ....

3. What is the bird doing? ....

4. What is the girl giving to the bear? an ....

5. Where is the bird now? on the bear's ....

G Listen to your teacher and point. Then draw lines.

H Listen and sing the song.
06

Jellyfish! Look, jellyfish!
And sandfish, happy sandfish
Swim, swim, swim
in the sea!

Goatfish! Look, goatfish!
And cowfish, funny cowfish
Live in the water,
not in a tree!

Catfish! Look, catfish!
And dogfish, scary dogfish
Swim, swim, swim
in the sea!

Sunfish! Look, sunfish!
And starfish, little starfish
Love being in the water,
like you and me!

Accompanying audio tracks can be found on Presentation plus or online.

Let's Say!
Optional pronunciation practice at the back of the Student's Book focuses on initial key sounds to develop early speaking skills. Supported by accompanying audio.

Let's speak!
Optional extra speaking practice at the back of the Student's Book allows learners to practise the language needed for the Speaking part of the Cambridge English: Starters test.

How could teachers use *Storyfun 2*?

1. Encourage learners to predict the general topic of the story using flashcards and the story pictures.
2. Teach or revise any Cambridge English: Starters words that are important in the story.
3. Play the audio or read the story.
4. (Optional) Discuss the story 'value' with learners. You will probably need to do this in your learners' first language to fully explore what the story teaches the reader.
5. Present the vocabulary and general comprehension tasks (usually Activities A–C).
6. Present the grammar, vocabulary and skills sections (generally Activities D–H).
7. Encourage collaborative learning with the 'Let's have fun!' at the back of the Student's Book.
8. Follow communicative pair or group work suggestions in the 'Let's speak!' pages at the back of the Student's Book.
9. Use extension activities in the Teacher's Book or set homework tasks.

How is the Teacher's Book organised?

Main topics and grammar

Cambridge English: Starters topics and grammar focused on in the activities in this unit.

Story summary

Main vocabulary

Cambridge English: Starters vocabulary focused on in the activities in this unit.

✔️ **Test tasks for Starters**

Authentic activities that follow the exact format of Cambridge English: Starters test tasks.

➡️ **Practice for Starters**

Specific activities that gently build up learners' familiarity and practise for the Cambridge English: Starters test.

Equipment

Any equipment or materials needed for teaching the unit, including photocopiables, digital flashcards, audio.

Storytelling

Extended notes for approaching storytelling with your learners give detailed suggestions on how to fully exploit digital resources and prompt meaningful and motivating discussions.

Value

The value can be explored and discussed with learners after reading the story. Discussion is optional, either directly after listening or when learners attempt the value activity.

Activity notes

A, B, C, etc. sections correspond to Student's Book activities.

IA Interactive activity

Activity that can also be completed interactively on Presentation plus.

Answer keys

Answers or suggested answers.

Extension activities

Flexible ideas to extend activities either in class or for homework.

Test tips and practice

Specific tips for the Cambridge English: Starters test with optional accompanying activity.

▶️ **Audio**

Track listing for accompanying audio on Presentation plus or online

Audioscripts

All scripts for listening activities in the Student's Book. Scripts for stories are not listed.

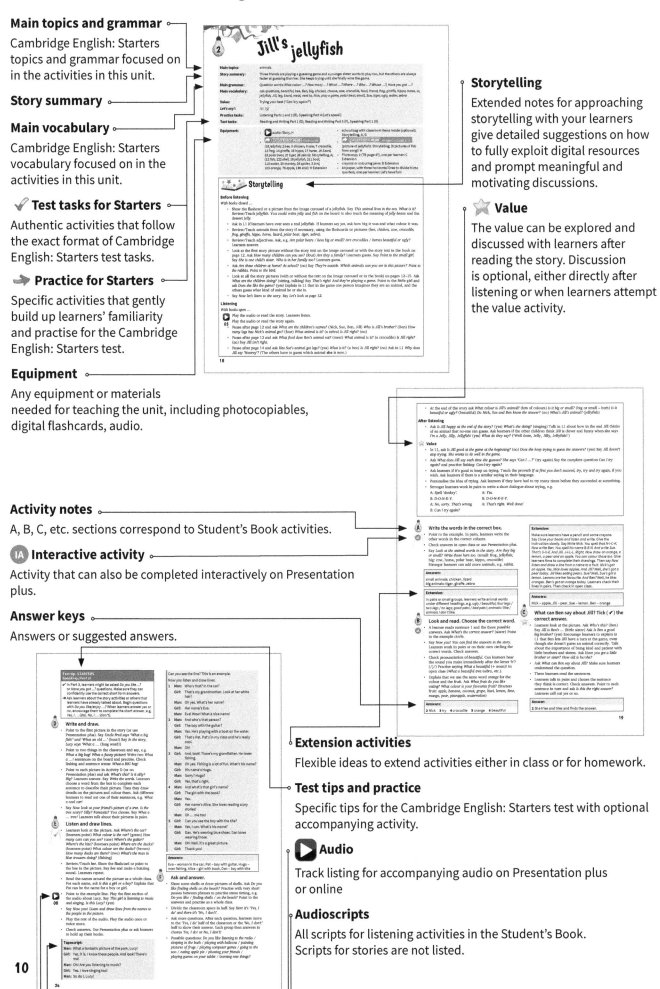

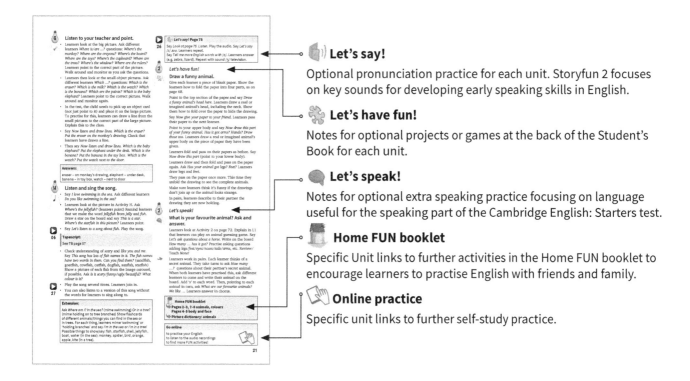

Let's say!

Optional pronunciation practice for each unit. Storyfun 2 focuses on key sounds for developing early speaking skills in English.

Let's have fun!

Notes for optional projects or games at the back of the Student's Book for each unit.

Let's speak!

Notes for optional extra speaking practice focusing on language useful for the speaking part of the Cambridge English: Starters test.

Home FUN booklet

Specific Unit links to further activities in the Home FUN booklet to encourage learners to practise English with friends and family.

Online practice

Specific unit links to further self-study practice.

How is the digital organised?

Presentation plus

IA *Interactive activities*

Every 'Activity A' in each unit is interactive to check vocabulary comprehension after reading the story and encourage whole-class participation. Other IA activities can be used as a supporting feature, either as a means of introducing an activity, scaffolding, or during answer feedback.

 Audio

Audio can be launched from the audio icon. Accompanying audioscripts can be displayed on screen.

Answer key

All activities have a visual answer key to easily display and check answers with your learners.

Digital flashcards

All Cambridge English: Starters test words are supported with visual flashcards with accompanying audio. Ideas for how these can be used are detailed in the teacher's notes for each unit.

Image carousel

These additional images can be used to prompt further discussion on themes and concepts. Ideas of when and how to use them are within the teacher's notes for each unit.

Each story also has a collection of separate images of the Student's Book pictures without text to prompt discussion before learners open their books and listen, revise the story if heard in a previous lesson or to use as a wrapping-up activity where learners can re-tell the story they've listened to.

Online practice

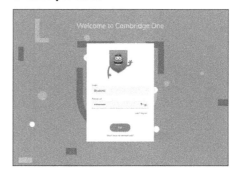

For the teacher
o   Presentation plus
o   All audio recordings
o   Additional digital resources to support your classes

For the student
o   Fun activities to practise the exam, skills and language
o   All audio recordings
o   Additional digital resources

Word FUN World app

Checklist for Cambridge English: Starters

Storyfun 2 provides learners with examples of all Cambridge English: Starters test tasks.

Paper	Part	Task	Unit
Listening 20 minutes 20 questions	1	Draw lines between names and people inside a picture.	Practice: 2 Test: 3, 7
	2	Write numbers and spellings of names.	Practice: 1, 2 Test: 4, 5
	3	Multiple choice. Tick the correct picture.	Practice: 5 Test: 1, 6, 8
	4	Follow instructions and colour parts of a picture.	Test: 3, 8
Reading and Writing 20 minutes 25 questions	1	Put a tick or cross to show whether the sentence is correct or not for a picture.	Practice: 4 Test: 2, 6
	2	Write *yes* or *no* to show whether a sentence about a picture is true or false.	Test: 1, 8
	3	Write words, using given jumbled letters, next to a picture.	Practice: 6 Test: 1, 7
	4	Gap fill about an illustrated subject. Write one noun in each gap.	Practice: 4 Test: 3, 5
	5	Write one-word answers to questions about three scene pictures.	Practice: 5 Test: 2, 8
Speaking 3–5 minutes	1	Point to parts of a picture and place object cards in the correct place.	Practice: 1 Test: 2, 7
	2	Answer questions about the picture.	Practice: 1, 3, 6, 7
	3	Answer questions about the remaining object cards.	Practice: 3 Test: 4
	4	Answer personal questions.	Practice: 1, 2, 3, 4, 5, 6, 7, 8

Map of the Student's Book

Story and Unit	Value	Topics	Grammar	Test tasks for Starters
1 Our funny home	Loving your family and home ("*I love my family. I love my home.*")	home	prepositions: *under, in, on, in front of, next to, behind, between* *There is/are …* *Where's …?*	Reading and Writing Parts 2 and 3 Listening Part 3
2 Jill's jellyfish	Trying your best ("*Can I try again?*")	animals	question words: *What colour …?, How many …?, Which …?, Where …?, Who …?, Whose …?* *Have you got …?*	Reading and Writing Parts 1 and 5 Speaking Part 1
3 Uncle Fred and me	Enjoying a varied and active life ("*I love -ing.*")	activities natural world	*like/love + ing* *What a (big) (fish)!*	Reading and Writing Part 4 Listening Parts 1 and 4
4 Mrs Day's garden	Making amends ("*Would you like to … with me?*")	farm animals clothes	*There is/are* present continuous	Listening Part 2 Speaking Part 3
5 Classmates	Celebrating diversity ("*I don't. / So do I.*")	school activities	present continuous *(The children / They are …-ing. The monster isn't …-ing. It's …-ing.)*	Listening Part 2 Reading and Writing Part 4
6 I want that game!	Being kind ("*Don't worry.*")	transport	*mine, yours, his, hers, theirs, ours* *this/that, these/those*	Reading and Writing Part 1 Listening Part 3
7 Monkey beach	Being happy ("*Be happy.*")	leisure	*have + noun + to …* (*She has some juice to drink.*) present continuous	Listening Part 1 Reading and Writing Part 3 Speaking Part 1
8 Winners!	Working as a team ("*I'm good at …*")	sport	question words: *What colour …?, How many …?, Which …?, Where …?, Who …?, Whose …?* *Have you got …?*	Reading and Writing Parts 2 and 5 Listening Parts 3 and 4

Our funny home

Main topics:	home
Story summary:	A boy describes his funny home and talks about his family and unusual pets.
Main grammar:	prepositions: *under, in, on, in front of, next to, behind, between, There is/are ..., Where's ...?*
Main vocabulary:	*apartment/flat, armchair, bath, bathroom, bed, bedroom, bookcase, box, cat, chairs, clean, coconut, cupboard, Dad, dining room, door, ducks, family, floor, frogs, Grandma, Grandpa, hall, hippo, house, kitchen, lamp, living room, lizard, mirror, Mum, painting, picture, pineapple, radio, rooms, table, wall, watch, window*
Value:	Loving your family and home (*"I love my family. I love my home."*)
Let's say!:	/eɪ/ /əʊ/ /aɪ/
Practice tasks:	Speaking Part 4 (C), Listening Part 2 (E), Speaking Part 2 (F)
Test tasks:	Reading and Writing Part 3 (D), Reading and Writing Part 2 (F), Listening Part 3 (G)

Equipment:	
	• ▶ audio: Story, G • presentation **PLUS** flashcards (117 *bathroom*, 119 *bedroom*, 127 *dining room*, 131 *hall*, 133 *kitchen*, 135 *living room*; 122 *chair*, 116 *bath*, 128 *door*, 159 *floor*, 155 *bookcase*, 143 *table*, 146 *wall*, 118 *bed*, 147 *window*, 125 *cupboard*, 144 *TV*, 134 *lamp*, 123 *clock*, 124 *computer*, 126 *desk*; 115 *armchair*, 141 *rug*): Storytelling, A, B, D, Let's speak!; (111 *sweets*, 87 *fries/chips*, 106 *pie*): E	• ➡ presentation **PLUS** Image carousel 1–11 (6 pictures of rooms): A, (5 pictures of families and their homes): Storytelling, H • Photocopy 1 (TB page 46), one per learner: D Extension • large pieces of coloured card (one per learner), furniture catalogues, scissors, glue, paper, crayons or colouring pens: Let's have fun!

Storytelling

Before listening

With books closed ...

- Show photographs of two homes from the Image carousel. Point and say, e.g. *Look! This is a ...* (home/house/flat/apartment) Ask *Do you live in a house or a flat? Do you live with your grandpa/brother/sister? How many people are there in your family?*
- Show flashcards of rooms or use pictures from the Image carousel to review/teach *bathroom, bedroom, dining room, hall, kitchen* and *living room*. Review/Teach with flashcards *chair, bath, door, floor, bookcase, table, wall, bed, window, cupboard, TV* and *lamp*. Point to the furniture on flashcards or in the classroom and ask *What's this?*
- Review/Teach prepositions (*under, in, in front of, next to, behind, on, between*) using flashcards or classroom objects.
- Look at the first story picture without the story text on the Image carousel or with the story text in the book on page 4. Ask *What room is this? A bedroom? A kitchen?* Learners guess. Ask *Where's the cat? Where's the window? Where's the radio? Where are the oranges?* (learners point) *And can you see a table? A book? A mouse?* Learners answer.
- Learners look at the other pictures (with or without the text on the Image carousel or in the book) on pages 5–7. Ask *What room is this? What can you see here?*
- Say *Now let's listen to the story.* Say *Let's look at page 4.*

Listening

With books open ...

▶ Play the audio or read the story. Learners listen.

02 Play the audio or read the story again.

- Pause after page 4 and say *So, what's this room? It's a ...* (kitchen) *How many oranges can you see?* (ten) *Is it a funny kitchen?* (yes)
- Halfway through page 5 ask *Who's in the bath?* (Grandma) *What animals are in the bathroom?* (ducks) *How many boats are there?* (four) *Where are they? On the ...* (floor) Ask *Is your bathroom at home like this?*
- At the end of page 5 ask *What's under the TV?* (a lizard) *What colour is it?* (green) *There's a grey animal here too. What is it?* (a hippo) *Is it big or is it a baby?* (a baby) Ask *Is there a hippo in your living room?* (no!)
- Pause after page 6. Point to the teeth and ask *Are these Mum's teeth?* (no! Grandpa's)
- At the end of the story ask *Where does the pet snake sleep?* (on the computer) *How many shoes are under the bed?* (12) *Is it a funny home?* (yes)

After listening

- Talk about the story (in L1 if necessary). Ask *What animals are there in the story?* (a cat, ducks, frogs, a lizard, a hippo, a snake, a dog, a mouse) *Is this house like a zoo?* (yes!)
- Ask *Would you like to live in this house?* Learners explain why / why not in L1.

 Value

- To be able to fully explore the story message with learners, discuss its value in L1.
- Point to the boy in the picture on page 7 and ask *Is he happy or sad?* (happy) *Does he like the house?* (yes) Say *That's right. He loves it. He says, 'I love my family and I love my ...'* (home) Practise word and sentence stress: *I LOVE my FAMily. I LOVE my HOME.*
- Say *The house in the story is different. The radio is in Mum's hat! There's a hippo in the living room. It's funny!* Ask why else this house is funny. Learners answer, e.g. *There are ducks in the bathroom!*
- Say *This child lives in a really funny home and his family do really funny things, but he loves his home and he loves his ...* (family) In L1 explain that every home and family is different and that's fine! Encourage learners to add their opinions to this discussion.
- Ask *How many people live in your house? Have you got a dining room? Have you got a pet? Does it live in the house?*

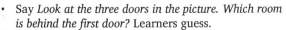

A Draw lines.

- Say *Look at the three doors in the picture. Which room is behind the first door?* Learners guess.
- Say *I'm behind the second door.* Mime making a cake. Ask *Where am I?* Learners guess (in the kitchen). Ask stronger learners *What am I doing?* (making a cake) Say *Well done! I make cakes in the kitchen.* Repeat, with mimes for *watch TV, eat, clean my face and hands.*
- Do the example. Point to the first sentence and say *I go to bed and sleep in my ...* (bedroom) Say *Look at the line.* Say *Now you!* Learners draw lines.
- Check answers in open class or use Presentation plus.
- Ask *Where am I? I'm eating with my family ...* (in the dining room) *And now? I'm cleaning my face and hands ...* (in the bathroom)

Answers:

2 a   3 b   4 f   5 d   6 e

Extension:

Learners work in pairs. Learner A mimes an action for one room and asks *What am I doing? Where am I?* Learner B guesses the action, or the action and the room, e.g. *You're watching TV. / You're watching TV in the living room!*

B Find the words and write.

- Read the questions in Activity B. Ask learners in L1 to think about what kind of word they need for the answer, e.g. *Who?* (a name) *How many?* (a number) *Where?* (a place) *What?* (a thing)
- Do the example. Show learners that all the answers are in the 'word wall'.
- Learners circle the words in the word wall and write them in the gaps. Check answers.

Answers:

2 Grandma   3 tree   4 lizard   5 eleven/11   6 green

C Which boy is correct? Read and tick (✔) the box.

- Learners look at the pictures. Use Presentation plus to show a large version if possible. Say *These three boys are talking about a story. Which boy is talking about **our** story?*
- Learners read the speech bubbles. In pairs, they talk and decide which boy is talking about 'Our funny home'. Learners compare their answer in pairs.
- Ask *Do you love your home? Who lives in your home? Have you got a garden? Where do you play? Do you like going to the zoo? What's your favourite animal?*

Answer:

Matt / picture 2

D Look at the pictures. Look at the letters. Write the words.

- With books closed, show the alphabet using Presentation plus or write it in large clear lower case letters on the board. Say the alphabet in open class and practise letters your learners find difficult.
- Ask stronger learners *How do you spell your name?* They spell their name aloud.
- If possible, show flashcards *armchair, lamp, window, rug, bed, desk.* Say, e.g. *Point to the armchair* or ask *What's this?*
- Open books and do the example. Point to the first picture and ask *What's this? It's a ...* (rug) Point to the jumbled letters and say *g-u-r. That's not right!* Explain in L1 that the letters are jumbled. Point to the answer and say *You spell 'rug' r-u-g.* Ask *How do you spell 'rug'?* Learners spell *rug* in chorus.
- Learners complete the activity in pairs.
- Check answers in open class or use Presentation plus.
- For each word, ask *How do you spell (bed)?* Learners say the letters in chorus.

Answers:

1 bed   2 lamp   3 desk   4 window   5 armchair

✔ In Part 3, learners look at a picture and then write its word. The letters for spelling the word are given but are jumbled.

→ Ask learners to write three or four more jumbled letter tasks for their classmates. In their notebooks, learners draw pictures of words from the Starters word list, e.g. a cat, a pencil, an apple, a robot, and then write the jumbled letters under each picture. They swap notebooks and write the correct spellings.

Extension: Photocopiable 1

Give each learner a photocopy of '1 The home' (TB page 46).
Learners look carefully at the picture and circle the correct words in the sentences. They check answers in pairs. Then check in open class. Different learners read out the correct sentences and the rest of the class point to the items in the picture.
Learners count the items in the picture and complete the sentences using *There are* and the correct numbers. Check answers in open class. Write the full sentences on the board.

Answers:

1 **2** mirror **3** rug **4** desk **5** flowers **6** bookcase
2 **2** There are 10 **3** There are 16 **4** There are 15
   5 There are 17 **6** There are 11

Listen and write the numbers.

• Write numbers *1–20* on the board and practise pronunciation. Show learners that *2, too* and *to / 4* and *for* sound exactly the same. Say the numbers in order with the whole class. Then point to individual numbers in a different order. Learners say the numbers.

• Say *Listen and write.* Say the numbers between *11* and *20* in a different order (e.g. *13, 19, 17, 12, 20, 18, 14, 11, 16, 15*). Learners write them (as figures, not words) in their notebooks. Repeat the numbers so they can check their answers. Check as a class.

• Learners look at the coloured numbers in Activity E. Ask *Which numbers are red?* (10, 11) *Yellow?* (3, 4) *Green?* (14, 19) *Purple?* (7, 15)

• Show flashcards of *sweets, fries* and *pie*. Ask *Do you like eating sweets? Fries? Pie? What's in your favourite pie?* Leave the flashcards on the board.

03

• Say *Listen and write numbers.* Play the audio twice if necessary. Pause after each number for learners to write (in pencil). Play the audio once or twice more.

• Check answers in open class or use Presentation plus.

• Read out the poem. Stop before each number. Learners call out the correct number before you continue.

Answers:

14 (shoes)   15 (games)   18 (toys)   13 (pencils)
20 (pens)   19 (sweets)   16 (fries)

Tapescript:

See SB page 10 and Answer key

Extension:

Write on the board *Oh dear! OK! Ben's! Great!* Divide the class into four groups. The first group reads out the first verse of the poem in chorus. Point to *Oh dear!* The rest of the class calls out *Oh dear!* Continue in the same way with verses 2, 3 and 4.

Look and read. Write *yes* or *no*.

Learners look at the picture. Say *Look! It's the funny home from our story!* Point to the balloon and ask *What's this?* (a balloon) *What colour is the balloon?* (yellow) *Where's the donkey?* (learners point) *Where's the hippo?* (learners point) *How many windows can you see?* (12) *What's the girl doing?* (smiling / playing football)

• Say *The bird is in a tree. Yes or no?* (no) Say *Well done! The bird is flying. There are two children. Yes or no?* (yes)

• Two learners read the examples. Learners point to the door and the bird.

• Learners read sentences 1–5 on their own and write *yes* or *no.*

• Check answers in open class. If using Presentation plus, ask learners to show you how they found the answer (they point to the correct part of the picture). Stronger learners can correct the wrong sentences.

• You can create more activities like this. Use pictures from the Image carousel, flashcards or magazines.

Answers:

1 no **2** yes **3** no **4** yes **5** no

Extension:

With stronger learners, ask questions about the picture to get them to use their imaginations:
What's the girl saying to the boy? What's the boy's answer? What's the girl saying to the donkey? What's the donkey's answer?
What's the boy saying to the hippo? What's the hippo's answer?
What's the bird saying to the girl? What's the girl's answer?
Learners discuss their answers in pairs.

Listen and tick (✔) the box.

Learners read each question and look at the possible picture answers. Check understanding by asking *What can you see in this picture? And in this one? And here?* Play the audio and pause after the example. Ask *Which picture shows Mark's flat? Can you see the tick?* (A) *What colour are its walls?* (white) *Are its windows big or small?* (small)

04

• Learners listen to the rest of the audio and tick answers with a pencil. Play the audio a second time. Learners check and complete their answers. If necessary, play the audio again.

• Alternatively, do this activity as a test rather than as a practice. Give learners a minute or so to read the questions and look at the possible answers before you play the audio twice. Learners listen and tick their answers.

• Check answers in open class or use Presentation plus.

Answers:

1 B **2** B **3** B **4** A **5** C

Tapescript:

Which is Mark's flat?

Boy: There's Mark's flat, Mum. The white one.

Woman: The one with the big grey windows?

Boy: No. Mark's flat has got small windows.

Woman: Oh! I see.

Can you see the tick? Now you listen and tick the box.

1 Where are Anna's new pens?

Girl: Where are my pens, Mum? Are they on that chair?

Woman: No, Anna. They're under the chair.

Girl: OK. Oh ... and here are my pencils – behind the chair!

Woman: Good!

2 Who is Grace phoning now?

Boy: Grace? Grace? Who are you phoning now?

Girl: Sshh. My new friend. He's learning English.

Boy: Oh! Is your mother giving him lessons?

Girl: No. My grandfather.

3 What is in the baby's bath?

Girl: What's the baby got in his bath, Mum? His toy fish?

Woman: Not today. He's got his toy duck.

Girl: And his toy ship?

Woman: No. That's on the floor!

4 Where is the cat?

Boy: Where is the cat, Dad? I can't find it.

Man: Well, it isn't on the sofa.

Boy: Is it on the bookcase again?

Man: No. Oh! There it is. It's in the cupboard.

5 Which is Grandmother's T-shirt?

Boy: Is this Grandmother's T-shirt?

Woman: Has it got the number 15 on it?

Boy: No, the number 19.

Woman: Yes, that's hers. And the one with the number 17 is for you!

Boy: Wow! Thanks!

Choose the words for you.

- Write *pineapple* and *flat* on the board. Point and say *I live in a pineapple. Is that right? Yes or no?* (no!) Say *I live in a flat.* Circle the word *flat.*

- Say *Now you!* Learners read the sentences and circle the words that are right for them. Explain that they can circle more than one word in each sentence if they like, e.g. *bed* and *desk* in the second sentence. Write *bed desk* on the board. Insert *and* to show learners they need to put *and* before the last word if they include more than one word.

- Learners say their own sentences in pairs, e.g. *I live in a flat. There is a bed and an armchair in my bedroom. There are flowers, lamps and rugs in our living room. There is a mirror and a bath in our bathroom.* Check that they are using *There is/are* and articles (*a/an*) correctly.

- Ask some learners to read out their sentences. With stronger learners, ask questions, e.g. *What colour is the armchair in your bedroom? Is the mirror in your bathroom big or small?*

26

🔊 *Let's say!* **Page 74**

Say *Look at page 74. Listen.* Play the audio. Say *Let's say* /eɪ/ *train.* Learners repeat.
Say *Tell me more English words with* /eɪ/. Learners answer (e.g. painting, radio). Repeat with sounds /əʊ/ *boat* (e.g. coconut, hippo) and /aɪ/ *kite* (e.g. dining room, pineapple).

Let's have fun!

Design your dream bedroom.

In L1 explain that learners are going to make a picture of their dream bedroom. Say *Close your eyes. What is in your dream bedroom? Is there a big bed or a small bed? What colour is it? How many windows are there? Is there a bookcase? Is there a big cupboard for your toys? Is there a rug? What colour is it? Have you got any pets in your dream bedroom? A rabbit? A lizard? A hippo?*

Give each learner a large piece of coloured card, furniture catalogues, scissors, glue, paper and crayons. They make a picture of their dream bedroom, as on page 68. They cut out pictures or draw and colour them and label the things.

Learners show their pictures and talk about their bedroom, e.g. *This is my dream bedroom. It has got a blue bed and two windows. There is a big rug and a white desk. There are some fish. They are orange and purple.*

Stronger learners can write sentences about their dream bedroom.

Let's speak!

Where is it? Play a game.

Ask learners to turn to page 72 in their Student's Book and look at Activity 1.
Review/Teach prepositions using the flashcards or things in the classroom.

Read the speech bubbles and explain the game in L1 if necessary.

Divide learners into pairs. Learner A chooses a thing in the classroom which he/she can say in English. He/She does not look at the object (it has to be secret from their partner). Learner B guesses its position, e.g. *Is it next to the door? Is it under the window?* Learner A answers *Yes* or *No.*

📦 **Home FUN booklet**
➡ **Pages 10–11, 14–15, 24–25 family, home, numbers**
➡ **Picture dictionary: home**

Go online

to practise your English
to listen to the audio recordings
to find more FUN activities!

Jill's jellyfish

2

Main topics:	animals
Story summary:	Three friends are playing a guessing game and a younger sister wants to play too, but the others are always faster at guessing than her. She keeps trying until she finally wins the game.
Main grammar:	question words: *What colour …? How many …? Which …? Where …? Who …? Whose …?, Have you got …?*
Main vocabulary:	*ask questions, beautiful, bee, Ben, big, chicken, choose, cow, crocodile, food, friend, frog, giraffe, hippo, horse, in, jellyfish, Jill, leg, lizard, meat, next to, Nick, play a game, polar bear, small, Sue, tiger, ugly, water, zebra*
Value:	Trying your best (*"Can I try again?"*)
Let's say!:	/z/ /ʒ/
Practice tasks:	Listening Parts 1 and 2 (B), Speaking Part 4 (Let's speak!)
Test tasks:	Reading and Writing Part 1 (D), Reading and Writing Part 5 (F), Speaking Part 1 (G)
Equipment:	<ul><li>▶ audio: Story, H</li><li>➡ (presentation **PLUS**) flashcards (18 *jellyfish*, 2 *bee*, 5 *chicken*, 6 *cow*, 7 *crocodile*, 13 *frog*, 14 *giraffe*, 16 *hippo*, 17 *horse*, 19 *lizard*, 23 *polar bear*, 27 *tiger*, 28 *zebra*): Storytelling, A; (12 *fish*, 222 *shell*, 18 *jellyfish*, 211 *boat*, 113 *water*, 20 *monkey*, 26 *spider*, 3 *bird*, 103 *orange*, 79 *apple*, 186 *kite*): H Extension</li></ul>	<ul><li>school bag with classroom items inside (optional): Storytelling, A, G</li><li>➡ (presentation **PLUS**) Image carousel 12–20 (picture of jellyfish): Storytelling; (8 pictures of fish from song): H</li><li>Photocopy 2 (TB page 47), one per learner: C Extension</li><li>crayons or colouring pens: B Extension</li><li>A4 paper, with three horizontal lines to divide it into quarters, one per learner: Let's have fun!</li></ul>

 ## Storytelling

Before listening

With books closed …

- Show the flashcard or a picture from the Image carousel of a jellyfish. Say *This animal lives in the sea. What is it?* Review/Teach *jellyfish*. You could write *jelly* and *fish* on the board to also teach the meaning of *jelly beans* and the dessert *jelly*.
- Ask in L1 if learners have ever seen a real jellyfish. If learners say *yes*, ask how big it was and what colour it was.
- Review/Teach animals from the story if necessary, using the flashcards or pictures (*bee, chicken, cow, crocodile, frog, giraffe, hippo, horse, lizard, polar bear, tiger, zebra*).
- Review/Teach adjectives. Ask, e.g. *Are polar bears / bees big or small? Are crocodiles / horses beautiful or ugly?* Learners answer.
- Look at the first story picture without the story text on the Image carousel or with the story text in the book on page 12. Ask *How many children can you see?* (four) *Are they a family?* Learners guess. Say *Point to the small girl.* Say *She is one child's sister. Who is in her family too?* Learners guess.
- Ask *Are these children at home? At school?* (no) Say *They're outside. Which animals can you see in this picture? Point to the rabbits. Point to the bird.*
- Look at all the story pictures (with or without the text on the Image carousel or in the book) on pages 12–15. Ask *What are the children doing?* (sitting, talking) Say *That's right! And they're playing a game.* Point to the little girl and ask *Does she like the game?* (yes) Explain in L1 that in the game one person imagines they are an animal, and the others guess what kind of animal he or she is.
- Say *Now let's listen to the story.* Say *Let's look at page 12.*

Listening

With books open …

 Play the audio or read the story. Learners listen.

05 Play the audio or read the story again.

- Pause after page 12 and ask *What are the children's names?* (Nick, Sue, Ben, Jill) *Who is Jill's brother?* (Ben) *How many legs has Nick's animal got?* (four) *What animal is it?* (a zebra) *Is Jill right?* (no)
- Pause after page 13 and ask *What food does Ben's animal eat?* (meat) *What animal is it?* (a crocodile) *Is Jill right?* (no) Say *Jill isn't right.*
- Pause after page 14 and ask *Has Sue's animal got legs?* (yes) *What is it?* (a bee) *Is Jill right?* (no) Ask in L1 *Why does*

Jill say 'Hooray'? (The others have to guess which animal **she** is now.)

- At the end of the story ask *What colour is Jill's animal?* (lots of colours) *Is it big or small?* (big or small – both) *Is it beautiful or ugly?* (beautiful) *Do Nick, Sue and Ben know the answer?* (no) *What's Jill's animal?* (jellyfish)

After listening

- Ask *Is Jill happy at the end of the story?* (yes) *What's she doing?* (singing) Talk in L1 about how in the end Jill thinks of an animal that no-one can guess. Ask learners if the other children think Jill is clever and funny when she says *I'm a Jelly, Jilly, Jellyfish!* (yes) *What do they say?* ('Well done, Jelly, Jilly, Jellyfish!')

 Value

- In L1, ask *Is Jill good at the game at the beginning?* (no) *Does she keep trying to guess the answers?* (yes) Say *Jill doesn't stop trying. She wants to do well in the game.*
- Ask *What does Jill say each time she guesses? She says 'Can I …?'* (try again) Say the complete question *Can I try again?* and practise linking: *Can-I-try again?*
- Ask learners if it's good to keep on trying. Teach the proverb *If at first you don't succeed, try, try and try again,* if you wish. Ask learners if there is a similar saying in their language.
- Personalise the idea of trying. Ask learners if they have had to try many times before they succeeded at something.
- Stronger learners work in pairs to write a short dialogue about trying, e.g.

  A: *Spell 'donkey'.*   A: *Yes.*

  B: *D-O-N-K-Y.*   B: *D-O-N-K-E-Y.*

  A: *No, sorry. That's wrong.*   A: *That's right. Well done!*

  B: *Can I try again?*

 ## A Write the words in the correct box.

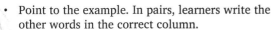

- Point to the example. In pairs, learners write the other words in the correct column.
- Check answers in open class or use Presentation plus.
- Say *Look at the animal words in the story. Are they big or small? Write those here too.* (small: frog, jellyfish; big: cow, horse, polar bear, hippo, crocodile) Stronger learners can add more animals, e.g. *rabbit.*

Answers:

small animals: chicken, lizard
big animals: tiger, giraffe, zebra

Extension:

In pairs or small groups, learners write animal words under different headings, e.g. *ugly / beautiful; four legs / two legs / no legs; good pets! / bad pets!; animals I like / animals I don't like.*

 ## B Look and read. Choose the correct word.

- A learner reads sentence 1 and the three possible answers. Ask *What's the correct answer?* (sister) Point to the example circle.
- Say *Now you! You can find the answers in the story.* Learners work in pairs or on their own circling the correct words. Check answers.
- Check pronunciation of *beautiful.* Can learners hear the sound you make immediately after the letter 'b'? (/j/) Practise saying *What a beautiful (+ noun)!* in open class (*What a beautiful tree/zebra*, etc.).
- Explain that we use the same word *orange* for the colour and the fruit. Ask *What fruit do you like eating? What colour is your favourite fruit?* (Starters fruit: *apple, banana, coconut, grape, kiwi, lemon, lime, mango, pear, pineapple, watermelon*)

Answers:

2 Nick **3** try **4** crocodile **5** orange **6** beautiful

---

 Extension:

Make sure learners have a pencil and some crayons. Say *Close your books and listen and write.* Give the instruction slowly. Say *Write Nick. You spell that N-I-C-K. Now write Ben. You spell his name B-E-N. And write Sue. That's S-U-E. And Jill. J-I-L-L. Right. Now draw an orange, a lemon, a pear and an apple. You can colour those too.* Give learners time to complete their drawings. Then say *Now listen and draw a line from a name to a fruit. Nick's got an apple. Yes, Nick loves apples. And Jill? Well, she's got a pear today. Jill likes eating pears. Sue? Well, Sue's got a lemon. Lemons are her favourite. And Ben? Well, he likes oranges. Ben's got an orange today.* Learners check their lines in pairs. Then check in open class.

Answers:

Nick – apple, Jill – pear, Sue – lemon, Ben – orange

 ## C What can Ben say about Jill? Tick (✔) the correct answer.

- Learners look at the picture. Ask *Who's this?* (Ben) Say *Jill is Ben's …* (little sister) Ask *Is Ben a good big brother?* (yes) Encourage learners to explain in L1 that Ben lets Jill have a turn at the game, even though she doesn't guess an animal correctly. Talk about the importance of being kind and patient with little brothers and sisters. Ask *Have you got a little brother or sister? How old is he/she?*
- Ask *What can Ben say about Jill?* Make sure learners understand the question.
- Three learners read the sentences.
- Learners talk in pairs and choose the sentence they think is correct. Check answers. Point to each sentence in turn and ask *Is this the right answer?* Learners call out *yes* or *no.*

Answer:

2 She tries and tries and finds the answer.

19

D Look and read. Put a tick (✔) or a cross (✘) in the box.

- Point to the first example. A learner reads the sentence. Ask *Is that right? Yes?* (draw a tick in the air) *No?* (draw a cross in the air). Learners say *Yes* and draw their own tick in the air. Repeat for the second example. Learners draw a cross in the air.

- Say *Now you! With your pencils, put a tick or a cross in the boxes.*

- Learners read the sentences and complete the activity.

- Copy the sentences on the board with the boxes next to them. Different learners come to the board and add a tick or cross for each sentence (or use Presentation plus).

- Learners can make true sentences for the sentences with crosses. (1 This is a girl. 3 This is fruit. 4 These are spiders.)

Answers:

1 ✘   2 ✔   3 ✘   4 ✘   5 ✔

Test tip: STARTERS
Reading and Writing (Part 1)

✔ In Part 1, learners put ticks or crosses in the boxes to show if sentences are right or wrong.

→ Practise answering using ticks or crosses. Give each learner two squares of card. They draw a tick on one card and a cross on the other. Show pictures of Starters words and say right or wrong sentences about the pictures, e.g. *This is a mouse* or *These are shoes*. Learners listen and hold up the correct card (the tick or the cross).
You could do this with four or five key words in each lesson.

E Look and read. Write the correct question word.

- Learners look at Activity E. Say *Point to the questions. Point to the answers.* (learners point)

- One learner reads the example question and another its answer. Show them that the question word has been crossed out in the word box. Say *Look at the answers. What are the correct question words?*

- Learners complete the questions in pairs.

- Check answers in open class or use Presentation plus.

Answers:

2 Who   3 Where   4 What   5 How many   6 Whose

F Look at the pictures and read the questions. Write one-word answers.

- Review/Teach the difference between *wearing* and *holding*, e.g. *What is Elena wearing on her feet? What is Massimo holding?* Learners answer. You could use pictures from the story or the Image carousel to ask more wearing/holding questions.

- Ask questions about the last story picture on page 15. Say *Answer with one word. How many children can you see?* (four) *What are the children doing? Are they sitting or standing?* (sitting) *Are they in a playground or a park? A …* (park) *What colour are Jill's shoes?* (pink)

- Learners look at the first picture in Activity F. Say *Now let's answer questions about this story. Listen and point. Where's the bear/tree/bird/girl?* (learners point) Do the examples with the class. Point to each answer. Ask *How many words are there in this answer?* (one) Say *Read the questions. Write one word in your answers.* Check learners understand that the questions refer to the picture **above** each time.

- Learners read the questions and write their answers. They compare answers in pairs.

- Check answers in open class or use Presentation plus.

Answers:

1 one/1   2 flowers   3 flying   4 apple   5 head

Test tip: STARTERS
Reading and Writing (Part 5)

✔ In Part 5, learners see three pictures which tell a short story. They then answer five questions about the pictures. Sometimes a question asks about an activity, e.g. *What is the monkey doing now?* Tell learners to answer that kind of question with an *-ing* word (e.g. *eating*).

→ Ask learners lots of questions about the story pictures – numbers of animals/trees, etc., where people are and what they are doing/holding/wearing, etc.

Listen to your teacher and point.

- Learners look at the big picture. Ask different learners *Where is/are ...?* questions: *Where's the monkey? Where are the crayons? Where's the board? Where are the toys? Where's the cupboard? Where are the trees? Where's the window? Where are the rulers?* Learners point to the correct part of the picture. Walk around and monitor as you ask the questions.

- Learners then look at the small object pictures. Ask different learners *Which ...?* questions: *Which is the eraser? Which is the milk? Which is the watch? Which is the banana? Which are the paints? Which is the baby elephant?* Learners point to the correct picture. Walk around and monitor again.

- In the test, the child needs to pick up an object card (not just point to it) and place it on the large picture. To practise for this, learners can draw a line from the small pictures to the correct part of the large picture. Explain this to the class.

- Say *Now listen and draw lines. Which is the eraser? Put the eraser on the monkey's drawing.* Check that learners have drawn a line.

- Then say *Now listen and draw lines. Which is the baby elephant? Put the elephant under the desk. Which is the banana? Put the banana in the toy box. Which is the watch? Put the watch next to the door.*

Answers:

eraser – on monkey's drawing, elephant – under desk, banana – in toy box, watch – next to door

Listen and sing the song.

- Say *I love swimming in the sea.* Ask different learners *Do you like swimming in the sea?*

- Learners look at the picture in Activity H. Ask *Where's the jellyfish?* (learners point) Remind learners that we make the word *jellyfish* from *jelly* and *fish*. Draw a star on the board and say *This is a star. Where's the starfish in this picture?* Learners point.

- Say *Let's listen to a song about fish.* Play the song.

06 Tapescript:

See TB page 57

- Check understanding of *scary* and *like you and me.* Say *This song has lots of fish names in it. The fish names have two words in them. Can you find them?* (sandfish, goatfish, cowfish, catfish, dogfish, sunfish, starfish) Show a picture of each fish from the Image carousel, if possible. Ask *Is it scary/funny/ugly/beautiful? What colour is it?*

- Play the song several times. Learners join in.

27

- You can also listen to a version of this song without the words for learners to sing along to.

Extension:

Ask *Where am I? In the sea?* (mime swimming) *Or in a tree?* (mime holding on to tree branches) Show flashcards of different animals/things you can find in the sea or in trees. For each thing, learners mime 'swimming' or 'holding branches' and say *I'm in the sea* or *I'm in a tree!* Possible things to show/say: fish, starfish, shell, jellyfish, boat, water (in the sea); monkey, spider, bird, orange, apple, kite (in a tree).

26

Let's say! Page 75

Say *Look at page 75. Listen.* Play the audio. Say *Let's say /z/ zoo.* Learners repeat.
Say *Tell me more English words with /z/.* Learners answer (e.g. zebra, lizard). Repeat with sound /ʒ/ television.

Let's have fun!

Draw a funny animal.

Give each learner a piece of blank paper. Show the learners how to fold the paper into four parts, as on page 68.

Point to the top section of the paper and say *Draw a funny animal's head here.* Learners draw a real or imagined animal's head, including the neck. Show them how to fold over the paper to hide the drawing.

Say *Now give your paper to your friend.* Learners pass their paper to the next learner.

Point to your upper body and say *Now draw this part of your funny animal. Has it got arms? Hands? Draw those too.* Learners draw a real or imagined animal's upper body on the piece of paper they have been given.

Learners fold and pass on their papers as before. Say *Now draw this part* (point to your lower body).

Learners draw and then fold and pass on the paper again. Ask *Has your animal got legs? Feet?* Learners draw legs and feet.

They pass on the paper once more. This time they unfold the drawing to see the complete animals.

Make sure learners think it's funny if the drawings don't join up or the animal looks strange.

In pairs, learners describe to their partner the drawing they are now holding.

Let's speak!

What is your favourite animal? Ask and answer.

Learners look at Activity 2 on page 72. Explain in L1 that learners can play an animal guessing game. Say *Let's ask questions about a horse.* Write on the board *How many ... has it got?* Practise asking questions adding *legs/feet/eyes/noses/tails/arms,* etc. Review/Teach *None!*

Learners work in pairs. Each learner thinks of a secret animal. They take turns to ask *How many ...?* questions about their partner's secret animal. When both learners have practised this, ask different learners to come and write their animal on the board. Add 's' to each word. Then, pointing to each animal in turn, ask *What are our favourite animals? We like ...* Learners answer in chorus.

Home FUN booklet

Pages 2–3, 7–8 animals, colours
Pages 4–5 body and face

Picture dictionary: animals

Go online

to practise your English
to listen to the audio recordings
to find more FUN activities!

Uncle Fred and me

3

Main topics:	activities, natural world
Story summary:	A girl talks about her uncle and their favourite places and hobbies.
Main grammar:	*like/love + ing, What a (big) (fish)!*
Main vocabulary:	*alphabet, beach, birds, boats, boots, camera, clothes, eating, finding, fishing, flying a kite, happy, ice cream, jeans, jumping, Lucy, people, playing guitar, reading, riding a bike, running, sand, scary, sea, shells, socks, spelling, swimming, taking photos, walking, watching TV, Uncle Fred, wearing, words, Wow!*
Value:	Enjoying a varied and active life (*"I love -ing"*)
Let's say!:	/tʃ/ /dʒ/ /ŋ/ /h/
Practice tasks:	Speaking Part 2 (E), Speaking Part 4 (F)
Test tasks:	Listening Part 1 (E), Reading and Writing Part 4 (G), Listening Part 4 (H)

Equipment:	audio: Story, E, H	• crayons or colouring pens: G

* audio: Story, E, H
* **presentation PLUS** flashcards
  (121 *camera*, 144 *TV*, 180 *fishing*, 176 *bike*, 182 *guitar*; 222 *shell*): Storytelling; (2 *bee*): E
* **presentation PLUS** Image carousel 21–29
  (5 pictures of activities): Storytelling; (4 pictures of shells and underwater scenes): Storytelling, G, H

* crayons or colouring pens: G
* Photocopy 3 (TB page 48), one per learner: H Extension
* large piece of blue paper (A3), one per learner; templates of fish, mermaids, swimming children, jellyfish, shells for learners to draw around; white card, crayons or colouring pens, glitter, glue, stickers, digital camera, sticky tack (optional): Let's have fun!

Storytelling

Before listening

With books closed …

* Ask *What do you like doing? Do you like taking photos / watching TV / fishing / riding your bike / playing the guitar?* Show flashcards or the Image carousel to help understanding if necessary. Learners say *Yes / No / I like …* Answer learners with *Me too! / So do I! / Do you? Oh! I don't!*

* Draw two men on the board. Point to the first one and say *This is my father.* Point to the second one and say *This is my father's brother. He's my uncle.* Ask *Have you got an uncle? What's his name?*

* Review/Teach *park, lake.* Write *park* and *lake* on the board. Ask *What can you do at the park?* (skateboarding, running, playing) *What can you do in a lake?* (fish, swim) Teach *shell.* Show a real shell or the flashcard. Explain in L1 that a sea creature's shell grows as the sea creature gets bigger. A creature's shell is its safe home and protects it from dangers in the sea.

* Look at the first story picture without the story text on the Image carousel or with the story text in the book on page 20. Ask *What can you see?* (a man, a park, a lake, trees)

* Learners look at the story pictures. Ask *Where's the sea / guitar / yellow car / chocolate cake / bike? Where are the ducks?* (learners point)

* Ask *What is the story about?* (Accept suggestions in English or L1.)

* Say *Now let's listen to the story.* Say *Let's look at page 20.*

Listening

With books open …

 Play the audio or read the story. Learners listen.

Play the audio or read the story again.

07

* Pause after page 20 and ask *What does Uncle Fred watch on TV? Does he watch football?* (no, hockey) *What does he eat?* (chocolate cake) *Look! Has he got a fish?* (no, a boot)

* Pause after page 21 and say *Uncle Fred is in the park. What's he doing?* (singing) Say *Uncle Fred likes taking photos of his …* (car) Ask *What colour is his car?* (yellow) *What colour are his socks?* (purple and yellow) *Are they funny?* (yes) Say *Uncle Fred likes wearing silly …* (clothes)

* Pause after page 22 and ask *What has Lucy got?* (a kite) Point to the trampoline, mime jumping and say *Lucy loves j…* (jumping) Point to the books and say *Lucy loves …* (reading) Review/Teach *scary.* Say *Lucy likes reading scary stories. Do you like scary stories?*

- At the end of the story ask *Where are Uncle Fred and Lucy?* (at the beach) *What are they wearing on their feet? Shoes and …* (funny socks) *What's Uncle Fred holding?* (a shell) *What colour is it?* (white)

After listening

- Say *Close your books. What does Uncle Fred like doing?* Mime the activities from the story. Say, e.g. *Uncle Fred likes …* (fishing) *He likes …* (singing) *He likes playing the …* (guitar) *He likes eating …* (chocolate cake)
- Say *Now tell me about Lucy.* Learners say what they remember, e.g. *Lucy likes flying a …* (kite) *She likes riding …* (her bike) *She likes watching …* (birds) *She likes spelling …* (long words)
- Ask different learners *Do you like watching hockey on TV / playing the guitar / running / reading / fishing / watching birds?*

 Value

- In L1, ask learners if it makes them happier if they are doing lots of different things that they really enjoy doing. Is it important to have fun hobbies? What do they think? Which hobbies might make children happiest? Riding a bike, watching TV, reading funny stories, swimming in the sea? There's no correct answer of course.
- Point to the first two pictures in the story. Say *Look! Uncle Fred's in the park and in his boat on the …* (lake) *Is Uncle Fred happy?* (yes) Say *That's right! He likes running and …* (fishing) Point to the picture of Lucy on her bike. Say *Lucy says I like flying my new …* (kite) *and I like riding on my …* (bike)
- Say, e.g. *I love playing tennis.* Ask *What do you love doing?* Write answers on the board (e.g. *skateboarding, being with my friends, playing basketball/tennis*).

A   Write the words in the correct box.

- Mime jumping, running, spelling, watching TV, taking photos, reading, fishing, riding a bike and singing. Ask *What am I doing?* (learners answer)
- Do the example. Learners write the *-ing* words in the correct box.
- Check answers in open class or use Presentation plus.

Answers:

I like	spelling, reading, riding a bike
Uncle Fred likes	running, watching TV, taking photos, fishing, singing

Extension:

Write on the board:
Lucy likes eating pink ice cream and drawing really ugly monsters and reading very scary stories and singing silly songs too.
Divide learners into four groups. Point to the words on the board and direct groups to speak as quickly as they can and mime actions to their lines. Practise the actions first.
In chorus, group 1 says *Lucy likes eating pink ice cream* (miming eating ice cream). Group 2 says *and drawing really ugly monsters* (miming drawing in the air). Group 3 says *and reading very scary stories* (miming looking scared and holding a book). Group 4 says *and singing silly songs too.* (mime singing and smiling)
Repeat the activity twice, encouraging groups to speak faster each time. Then the whole class says all the lines with all the actions.

B   Look and read. Choose the correct word.

- Do the example in open class.
- Learners circle the correct words and then check their answers in pairs.
- Check answers in open class.

Answers:

2 hockey   3 chocolate cake   4 yellow   5 kite
6 bike   7 shells

Extension:

Write on the board:
Yes!   We don't know!
Say *Listen to ten questions about Uncle Fred. Say Yes! or We don't know!*
Ask the questions in a different order, pausing for learners to answer in chorus.
Yes answers: *Does Uncle Fred love fishing / taking photos of his car / sitting on the rocks / watching hockey on TV / singing in the rain?*
We don't know answers: *Does Uncle Fred like eating apple cake / swimming in the lake / wearing purple hats / playing the piano / walking with his dog?*

C   Write and draw lines.

- Review/Teach *like doing* and *love doing.* Draw the smiley face on the board and say *Lucy likes flying her kite.* Draw the heart on the board and say *Lucy loves jumping.*
- Write on the board *Lucy ☺ riding her bike. Lucy ♥ spelling long words.* Point to the sentences and practise. Learners say *likes* or *loves* to match the icons. They can draw a smile in the air for *likes* and a heart shape with their fingers for *loves* as they speak.
- Do the examples.
- Learners complete the sentences. Then they draw lines from the sentences to the pictures.
- Check answers.

Answers:

3 likes   4 loves   5 loves   6 likes   7 loves

What about you?

- Point to the picture and remind learners, in L1, that having different hobbies and living an active life makes us happy.
- In pairs, learners tell each other what they love doing. Encourage learners to answer with, e.g. *Me too! So do I! Great! Wow! Cool!*
- Point to the question *What about you?* Review/Teach *morning, afternoon* and *evening.* Learners complete the sentence with their own ideas. Ask different learners to read their sentences to the class.

Test tip: STARTERS
Speaking (Part 3)

✔ In Part 3, learners might be asked *Do you like…?* or *Have you got…?* questions. Make sure they can confidently use the correct short form answers.

→ Ask learners about the story activities or others that learners have already talked about. Begin questions with *Do you like/enjoy …?* When learners answer *yes* or *no*, encourage them to complete the short answer, e.g. *Yes, I …* (do). *No, I …* (don't).

Write and draw.

- Point to the first picture in the story (or use Presentation plus). Say *Uncle Fred says 'What a big fish!'* and *'What an old …'* (boot!) Say *In the story, Lucy says 'What a … (long word!)*

- Point to two things in the classroom and say, e.g. *What a big bag! What a funny picture!* Write two *What a …!* sentences on the board and practise. Check linking and sentence stress: *What-a BIG bag!*

- Point to each picture in Activity D (or on Presentation plus) and ask *What's this? Is it silly? Big?* Learners answer. Say *Write the words.* Learners choose a word from the box to complete each sentence to describe their picture. Then they draw details on the pictures and colour them. Ask different learners to read out one of their sentences, e.g. *What a cool car!*

- Say *Now look at your friend's picture of a tree. Is the tree scary? Silly? Fantastic?* You choose. Say *What a … tree!* Learners talk about their pictures in pairs.

Listen and draw lines.

- Learners look at the picture. Ask *Where's the car?* (learners point) *What colour is the car?* (green) *How many cars can you see?* (one) *Where's the guitar? Where's the kite?* (learners point) *Where are the ducks?* (learners point) *What colour are the ducks?* (brown) *How many ducks are there?* (two) *What's the man in blue trousers doing?* (fishing)

- Review/Teach *bee.* Show the flashcard or point to the bee in the picture. Say *bee* and make a buzzing sound. Learners repeat.

- Read the names around the picture as a whole class. For each name, ask *Is this a girl or a boy?* Explain that *Pat* can be the name for a boy or girl.

08

- Point to the example line. Play the first section of the audio about Lucy. Say *This girl is listening to music and singing. Is this Lucy?* (yes)

- Say *Now you! Listen and draw lines from the names to the people in the picture.*

- Play the rest of the audio. Play the audio once or twice more.

- Check answers. Use Presentation plus or ask learners to hold up their books.

Tapescript:

Man: What a fantastic picture of the park, Lucy!

Girl: Yes, it is. I know these people. And look! There's me!

Man: Oh! Are you listening to music?

Girl: Yes. I love singing too!

Man: So do I, Lucy!

Can you see the line? This is an example.

Now you listen and draw lines.

1 Man: Who's that? In the car?

   Girl: That's my grandmother. Look at her white hair!

   Man: Oh yes. What's her name?

   Girl: Her name's Eva.

   Man: Eva! Wow! What a nice name!

2 Man: And who's that person?

   Girl: The boy with the guitar?

   Man: Yes. He's playing with a boat on the water.

   Girl: That's Pat. Pat's in my class and he's really cool.

   Man: Oh!

3 Girl: And, look! There's my grandfather. He loves fishing.

   Man: Oh yes. Fishing is a lot of fun. What's his name?

   Girl: His name's Hugo.

   Man: Sorry? Hugo?

   Girl: Yes, that's right.

4 Man: And what's that girl's name?

   Girl: The girl with the book?

   Man: Yes.

   Girl: Her name's Alice. She loves reading scary stories!

   Man: Oh … me too!

5 Girl: Can you see the boy with the kite?

   Man: Yes, I can. What's his name?

   Girl: Dan. He's wearing blue shoes. Dan loves wearing those.

   Man: Oh! Well, it's a great picture.

   Girl: Thank you!

Answers:

Eva – woman in the car, Pat – boy with guitar, Hugo – man fishing, Alice – girl with book, Dan – boy with kite

Ask and answer.

- Show some shells or draw pictures of shells. Ask *Do you like finding shells on the beach?* Practise with very short pauses between phrases to practise stress timing, e.g. *Do-you like / finding shells / on the beach?* Point to the answers and practise as a whole class.

- Divide the classroom space in half. Say *Here it's 'Yes, I do'* and *there it's 'No, I don't'.*

- Ask more questions. After each question, learners move to the *'Yes, I do'* half of the classroom or the *'No, I don't'* half to show their answer. Each group then answers in chorus *Yes, I do!* or *No, I don't!*

- Possible questions: *Do you like listening to the radio / sleeping in the bath / playing with balloons / painting pictures of frogs / playing computer games / going to the zoo / eating apple pie / phoning your friends / playing games on your tablet / learning new things?*

Read. Choose a word from the box and write.

- Say *Read about music.* Point to the words in the word box. Ask *How many words can you see here?* (eight) Point to the gaps and ask *How many words do we need?* (five) Say *That's right!*

- Point to the example. Then say *Now you! Find the words and write them on the lines.*

- In pairs or on their own, learners complete the text. Check answers in open class or use Presentation plus.

Answers:

1 radios   2 songs   3 bath   4 guitar   5 lessons

Listen and colour.

- Learners look at the picture. Ask *Where's Lucy?* (learners point) *What's the boy in the boat doing?* (fishing) *What's walking next to Lucy?* (a duck)

09
- Play the audio. Pause after the first colouring. Ask *Where's that shell?* (in the water) *What colour is that shell now?* (purple)

- Make sure learners have yellow, pink, green, orange and red crayons, including other colours. Remind learners in L1 that they don't have to colour beautifully or the whole of each shell.

- Play the rest of the audio. Learners listen and colour. Play the audio a second time. Check answers.

Answers:

shell on hat – yellow, under chair – pink, next to duck – green, in Lucy's hand – orange, on boat – red

Tapescript:

Listen and colour. There is one example.

Woman: Look at this picture. It's Lucy at the beach.

Boy: There are lots of shells in it!

Woman: Yes, there are. One shell is in the sea.

Boy: Can I colour the shell in the sea purple?

Woman: Yes! Great! Thanks!

Can you see the purple shell? This is an example. Now you listen and colour.

1 **Woman:** Find the shell on the hat now.

   Boy: The shell on the hat? Oh! I can see it.

   Woman: Fantastic! Colour that shell yellow, please.

   Boy: OK!

2 **Boy:** What now?

   Woman: Colour the shell under the chair.

   Boy: OK. What colour?

   Woman: Colour it pink.

   Boy: The shell under the chair! Right!

3 **Woman:** And one shell is next to the duck!

   Boy: Sorry?

   Woman: Look! There's a shell next to the duck!

   Boy: Oh yes. Can I colour that shell green?

   Woman: Yes!

4 **Boy:** Can I colour the shell in Lucy's hand?

   Woman: The shell in Lucy's hand? Yes! Colour it orange.

   Boy: OK. I'm doing that now.

   Woman: Thank you.

5 **Woman:** Now colour the shell on the boat.

   Boy: OK. Can I colour it red?

   Woman: Yes. That's a good colour for the shell on the boat.

   Boy: Great! There!

   Woman: Fantastic! I love this picture now.

   Boy: So do I!

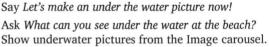

Let's say! Page 75

26
Say *Look at page 75. Listen.* Play the audio. Say *Let's say /tʃ/ chicken.* Learners repeat. Say *Tell me more English words with /tʃ/.* Learners answer (e.g. beach). Repeat with sounds /dʒ/ jeans (e.g. jump, jellyfish), /ŋ/ fishing (e.g. playing, reading) and /h/ hippo (e.g. happy, horse).

Let's have fun!

Make an underwater picture.

Say *Let's make an under the water picture now!*

Ask *What can you see under the water at the beach?* Show underwater pictures from the Image carousel. Write key words on the board (*shells, fish, rocks, jellyfish, starfish, old boats/ships*).

Give each learner a piece of blue paper and say *Make your underwater picture.* Learners make a large picture of non-moving items and three small pictures of moving items, as on page 69. They place the items on their picture and talk about their pictures in pairs.

Let's speak!

What do you love doing?

Learners look at Activity 3 on page 72. Ask two learners to read out the mini conversation. In L1, ask learners what the boy can say if he doesn't like swimming (I don't!) Under a tick on the board, write *Me too!* Under a cross, write *I don't!*

Learners work in pairs. They take turns to say *I love* ... or *I like* ... Their partner answers *Me too!* or *I don't.* Ask e.g. *What does (Marco) like doing?* Learners answer, e.g. *Playing football.* Ask *Do you like playing football, too?* Learners answer *Yes, I do. / No, I don't.*

Home FUN booklet
➡ **Pages 26–27 places**
➡ **Picture dictionary: activities**

Go online

to practise your English
to listen to the audio recordings
to find more FUN activities!

Mrs Day's garden

Main topics:	farm animals, clothes
Story summary:	The animals escape from a farm and go to a neighbour's garden, where they eat the fruit and vegetables and steal her laundry. Can the farmer make amends to his neighbour?
Main grammar:	*There is/are*, present continuous
Main vocabulary:	*angry, dirty, dress, garden, goats, Good morning, hat, home, look at, lunch, Mr, onions, open, sheep, shirt, skirt, T-shirt, wear*
Value:	Making amends (*"Would you like to … with me?"*)
Let's say!:	/aʊ/ /ɔɪ/
Practice tasks:	Reading and Writing Part 4 (C), Speaking Part 4 (F)
Test tasks:	Listening Part 2 (H), Speaking Part 3 (J)

Equipment:	audio: Story, E, G	• real phones, baseball caps and school bags (one item for each pair of learners): D
	➡ presentation **PLUS** flashcards	• Photocopy 4 (TB page 49), one per learner (optional): D Extension
	(6 *cow*, 24 *sheep*, 15 *goat*, 5 *chicken*, 10 *duck*, 81 *beans*, 102 *onion*, 104 *peas*, 105 *pear*, 108 *potato*): Storytelling	• piece of card (A3), one per group of three or four learners, magazines with photos of food, paper, crayons or colouring pens, glue, scissors: Let's have fun!
	• a real pear and some potatoes, peas, beans and onions: Storytelling, B Extension	
	➡ presentation **PLUS** Image carousel 30–39	
	(6 pictures of farm, farmer, gate, town, sweater): Storytelling; (2 pictures of restaurants, 2 pictures of menus): Let's have fun!	

★ ★ Storytelling

Before listening

With books closed …

- Show pictures from the Image carousel of a farm and a farmer. Write *farm* on the board. Add *-er* to show how to make *farmer*. You could add *teach/teacher* and *sing/singer*. Ask *Would you like to be a farmer one day?*

- Ask *Which animals can you see on a farm?* Write learners' suggestions on the board (cows, sheep, goats, chickens, ducks) and draw the animals or show flashcards. Ask *Which is your favourite farm animal?*

- Point to each animal word on the board. Learners make the animal sounds.

- Show flashcards of beans, onions, peas, pears and potatoes, or real foods. Ask *Which do you like eating?*

- Show the picture of a gate from the Image carousel. Ask *Is there a gate in our school?* Show the sweater. Ask *What colour is this sweater?*
Show the town. Say *You find homes and shops and schools here. It's a town.* In L1, you might like to add that a town is bigger than a village but smaller than a city.

- Look at the first story picture without the story text on the Image carousel or with the story text in the book on page 28. Ask *Where's the farm / the farmer? Can you see a garden / a woman / a truck?* (learners point) *What colour is the truck?* (blue) *What animals can you see?* (cows, sheep, dog) *Can you see any chickens?* (no)

- Look at all the story pictures (with or without the text on the Image carousel or in the book) on pages 12–15.

- Say *Now let's listen to the story.* Say *Let's look at page 28.*

Listening

With books open …

10

- Play the audio or read the story. Learners listen.

- Play the audio or read the story again.

- Pause at the end of page 28 and ask *What's the farmer's name?* (Mr Gray) *What's the woman's name?* (Mrs Day) Say *Mr Gray is going to the …* (town) *Is he in his car?* (no, his truck) *Mrs Day is going shopping. She's on the …* (bus)

- Pause after page 29 and ask *Are the gates open or closed?* (open) *Where are the animals?* (in Mrs Day's garden) Say *Oh dear!* Learners repeat.

- Pause after page 30 and ask *What are the animals eating now?* (potatoes, onions, peas, beans and pears) *What are the animals wearing?* (hats, T-shirts, shirts, dresses, sweaters and skirts)

A Look, count and write.

- Point to the first picture and ask *What animals can you see?* (sheep, cows, goats, a chicken) Say *Point to the beans / potatoes / onions.* Learners point to the correct basket.

- Look at the example. Ask *How many cows can you see?* (two) Learners look at the pictures and write numbers in the spaces.

- Check answers in open class or use Presentation plus.

Answers:

two sheep, two goats, two onions, three beans, four potatoes

B Look and number the pictures.

- Learners look at the pictures. Ask *Which picture starts the story?* Learners point to the picture of the farmhouse. Say *This is picture number 1. It starts the story.* Explain in L1 that learners need to order the pictures so they show the story. Then say *Now you! Write numbers in the boxes.*

- In pairs, learners write numbers to order the pictures.

Answers:

Left to right, learners number the pictures 5, (1), 2, 4, 3, 6

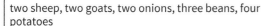

- Ask questions about each picture, to retell the story as a class: (1) *Mr Gray lives on a …* (farm) (2) *Today, Mr Gray and Mrs Day are going to …* (town) *Who's going on a bus?* (Mrs Day) *Yes, and Mr Gray is going in his …* (truck) (3) *Oh dear! The gates are …* (open) *Now the animals are in Mrs Day's …* (garden) (4) *What's the cow eating?* (a pear) (5) *What's the goat wearing?* (a hat) (6) *Is Mrs Day angry?* (yes) *What does Mr Gray say?* (Sorry)

Extension:

Divide learners into three groups. Give a story role to each learner (Mr Gray, Mrs Day and the farm animals). Tell the story and ask the groups to mime what's happening. You could use real fruit and vegetables. Mr Gray and Mrs Day join in with their lines and the animals make appropriate animal noises.

C Look, read and write.

- Ask *What's the farmer's name?* (Mr Gray) Point to the example and ask *Where are his animals? On his …* (farm). Check understanding of the other words.

- In pairs, learners read sentences 2–5 and write the answers.

Answers:

2 truck **3** bus **4** animals **5** clothes

- Review/Teach *There is … / There are …* Learners look at the first section of the story on page 28. Say *On Mr Gray's farm there are some …* (cows, sheep, goats, ducks and chickens) Point to the dog. Say *There is a …* (dog) Write *There are some cows* and *There is a dog* on the board.

- Say *You have a farm! What's on your farm?* Start your answers with 'There's' or 'There are'. Add learners' suggestions to the board, e.g. *There are some trees. There is a goat. There are some sheep. There are some chickens.* Teach *tractor* if that is useful. Learners could copy the sentences into their notebooks.

- Say the sentences. Add mimes, e.g make tree branch or moving tractor wheel shapes with your arms, or make animal noises. Learners say the sentences and copy your mimes / animal noises.

- Delete one word at a time from the sentences. Learners say the sentences including the missing words. Continue until they are saying the sentences from memory.

D Look and read. Say and answer.

- Point to the picture. Say *Look! Mrs Day is angry and Mr Gray is sorry. What does he say?* Learners read in chorus *'I am very sorry. Would you like to have dinner with me?'* In L1, talk about why Mr Gray is inviting Mrs Day to dinner. (He is sorry / feels bad / doesn't want to lose Mrs Day's friendship.)

- Write *Would you like …?* on the board. Knock an (unbreakable) item which belongs to a learner on the floor. Say *Oh dear! Are you angry?* The learner says *Yes!* Pick up the item and say *I am very sorry. Would you like an apple?* (offering a real/imagined apple) The learner says *Yes* and mimes taking the apple. Write *Would you like an apple?* on the board.

- Read the first sentence below the picture. Invite a confident learner to come and draw a frog sitting on a phone on the board. Add learners' suggestions for *Would you like …?* offers to the friend.

- In pairs or small groups, learners discuss and then role play the other situations.

E Listen and draw lines.

- Learners look at the picture. Say *Oh no! Where are Mr Gray's animals?* (in the garden)
- Point to the vegetables and say *What are these?* (onions, peas, potatoes, beans, pears)
- Say *Listen. What are the animals eating?*

11
- Play the audio. Pause after the example and say *Draw lines from the animals to the food.*
- Pause after each section for learners to draw lines. Play the recording once or twice more.
- Learners check answers in pairs. Check in open class or use Presentation plus.

Answers:

Learners draw lines: brown cow – beans, white sheep – onions, black and white cow – peas, chicken – potatoes, white goat – pears

Tapescript:

Girl: Oh no! Look! Mr Gray's animals are in Mrs Day's garden!

Boy: Yes! There's his grey goat. It's eating the flowers!

Girl: Oh dear! … Mrs Day! Mrs Day!

Boy: She's not here. She's in town today.

Can you see the line? This is an example. Now you listen and draw lines.

1 Girl: Look! There's Mr Gray's brown cow.
   Boy: Where? Oh … I can see it. It's eating the beans.
   Girl: Oh …

2 Girl: And that white sheep is eating her onions.
   Boy: It likes them! Look!

3 Girl: There's a black and white cow there, too.
   Boy: What's that cow eating?
   Girl: It's eating Mrs Day's peas.

4 Boy: And the chicken is eating her potatoes. Oh dear!

5 Girl: And that white goat … that white goat is eating the pears on her tree.
   Boy: Let's stop them!
   Girl: How?
   Boy: I don't know. Let's run and tell Mum! She can phone Mrs Day.

28

F Write and say.

- Review/Teach *breakfast, lunch, dinner*.
- Learners complete the sentences with the food they eat at different meals. They could add drinks too. Walk around and help with vocabulary.
- Learners compare sentences in pairs, e.g. *For breakfast, I eat bread and I drink milk.* Ask different learners *What does your friend eat?*

G Look, read and write.

- Review/Teach clothing if necessary (*dress, hat, shirt, skirt, T-shirt, sweater*).
- Learners look at the picture. Say *The animals are wearing clothes. What colour is the brown cow's skirt?* (blue) *What colour is the goat's sweater?* (pink) Review/ Teach *clean* and *dirty*. Ask *Are these clothes clean or dirty now?* (dirty)
- Do the example. Then learners write the words.
- Check answers.
- Ask *What's the brown cow / chicken thinking in this picture?* Encourage funny suggestions, e.g. *What a fantastic skirt! / This is my favourite hat!*

Answers:

2 T-shirt **3** shirt **4** hat **5** sweater **6** dress

H Read the questions. Listen and write a name or a number.

- Learners look at the picture and the examples. Ask *What is the boy's name?* (Mark) *How old is he?* (12) Say *Listen to Mark's cousin now. She's talking about Mark.*
- Learners read the questions quietly. For each question, ask *Is the answer a name or number?*

12
- Play the audio. Learners write the answers. Play the audio again. Learners compare their answers in pairs.
- Check answers in open class. Ask different learners to spell out the names.

Answers:

1 Show **2** Teddy **3** 16 **4** Fun **5** 8

Tapescript:

See TB pages 55–56

Test tip: STARTERS
Listening (Part 2)

✔ In Part 2, learners listen for information and then write names or numbers. The names are always spelled out.
➜ Practise numbers 1–20 and the alphabet. Ask learners to spell names and words from the Starters syllabus aloud so they get used to hearing the letters. Pay special attention to letters that your learners are likely to confuse, e.g. i/y/e, c/k, j/g, b/v, u/w, r/l.

I Look. Ask and answer.

- Review/Teach *play football, fish* (v), *read, sing, swim* and *watch TV* if necessary.
- Say *Look at the pictures.* Point to two or three different pictures and ask *What's he/she doing?* Learners answer (e.g. swimming, singing, playing football).
- Ask one pair of learners to read out the question and answer in the speech bubbles. Then closed pairs take turns to ask and answer the same question.

- Ask different learners to mime an activity. Ask the class *What's that boy/girl doing?* The class answers.

J. Look, listen and say.

- Say *Look and listen.* Point to each picture and ask the questions below. The first time, learners listen and think of their answers. Repeat the questions and choose learners to answer.

Questions:

What's this? Would you like to have a sheep? What's your favourite animal?
What are these? Have you got some boots? What are you wearing on your feet today?
What's this? Do you go to school on a bus? What colour is this bus?
What's this? Do you like onions? What do you like to eat for dinner?

Now draw and write. Then ask and answer.

Learners draw a picture of something from the story in the box. Then they complete the questions about their picture.

- Learners work in pairs. They take turns to show their picture and ask their questions.

Test tip: STARTERS
Speaking (Part 3)

✔ In Part 3, learners look at three object cards, e.g. a cake, a pen, a zebra. The examiner might ask *What's this? Do you like zebras?* and *What's your favourite animal?*

→ Make sure learners get used to answering closed questions (e.g. *Do you like cats?*) and open questions (e.g. *What colour's your T-shirt?*) about different animals, food or other words on the Starters word list.

▶ 🔊 *Let's say!* **Page 74**

26 Say *Look at page 74. Listen.* Play the audio. Say *Let's say* /aʊ/ **cow**. Learners repeat. Say *Tell me more English words with* /aʊ/. Learners answer (e.g. bounce, wow). Repeat with sound /ɔɪ/ **boy** (e.g. toy).

---

4. Let's have fun!

Make a menu.

Explain in L1 that you'd like learners to pretend they are going to open a restaurant. Teach *restaurant* and *menu*.

Divide the class into small groups. Say *Choose a name and a menu for your restaurant.*

Learners write their chosen name and food on a folded piece of card to make a menu, like the one on Student's Book page 69. They cut out pictures of food from magazines or draw food. They can add prices too (help them write prices in pounds).

Groups can use their menus to role play being waiters and customers. The waiter asks *Would you like (name of dish)?* The customer answers *Yes, please* or *No, thank you.*

---

4. Let's speak!

On the farm. Ask and answer.

Ask learners to turn to page 72 in their Student's Book and look at Activity 4.

Divide the class into groups A and B. To group A, say *You are farmers! What animals have you got on your farm? Don't tell us now!* To group B, say *You are coming to the farm. You'd like to ask questions about the farm and the animals.*

Learners then work in A and B pairs (one farmer, one visitor).

Write the following questions for the visitors on the board. They can also ask questions of their own. 'A's and 'B's swap roles, if there is time in your lesson.

Questions:

Is your farm big or small?

What animals live there?

What's your favourite animal?

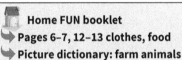

🏠 **Home FUN booklet**
➡ **Pages 6–7, 12–13 clothes, food**
➡ **Picture dictionary: farm animals**

Go online

to practise your English
to listen to the audio recordings
to find more FUN activities!

Classmates

5

Main topics:	school, activities
Story summary:	There is something unusual about one of the classmates in Mr Bath's class – he's a monster! He's sometimes naughty, but the other children love him anyway.
Main grammar:	present continuous (*The children / They are …-ing, The monster isn't …-ing. It's …-ing.*)
Main vocabulary:	*Anna, badminton, bags, baseball, basketball, beans, bread, children, chips, classmates, classroom, door, draw, drink, favourite, fish, football, Fred, hockey, listen, love, monster, paint (v), paper planes, play piano, read, Sam, see, shoe, sports, stories, street, table tennis, teacher, tennis, throw, wall, wave*
Value:	Celebrating diversity (*"I don't! / So do I!"*)
Let's say!:	/iː/ /ɑː/ /uː/
Practice tasks:	Reading and Writing Part 5 (D), Speaking Part 4 (F), Listening Part 3 (G)
Test tasks:	Listening Part 2 (C), Reading and Writing Part 4 (E)

Equipment:	
• audio: Story, C, G	• hat or bag and 12 pieces of paper with instructions: D Extension
• (presentation **PLUS**) flashcards (181 *football*): Storytelling	• Photocopy 5 (TB page 50), one per learner: D Extension
• (presentation **PLUS**) Image carousel 40–44 (3 pictures of classrooms around the world; 2 pictures of playgrounds): Storytelling	• large piece of paper, small pieces of coloured card, glue, crayons or colouring pens, scissors, feathers, stickers, etc. to make a collage (one set for each group of three or four learners): Let's have fun!

 ## Storytelling

Before listening

With books closed …

- Show photographs of classrooms and playgrounds from the Image carousel. Ask *What do you do in the classroom?* (read, write, listen, draw, paint, learn) *What do you do in the playground?* (run, talk, play games) *What sports do you play with a ball there?* Elicit *football/soccer* and explain that *football* is usually called *soccer* in American English.

- Say *It's the end of the school day. What am I doing?* Mime picking up your bag and going out of the door. Say *Picking up my …* (bag) *and going …* (home)

- Point to things in the classroom and ask *What's this?* (the door, a window, a pen, a book, the board, a poster, paper) Draw the story monster from page 36 on the board. Say *There's a monster in this story!*

- Look at the first story picture without the story text on the Image carousel or with the story text in the book on page 36. Say *Look at this classroom. How many children can you see?* (four) *Can you see some books?* (yes) *Can you see a door?* (no) *Where's the piano? Where's the clock?* (learners point)

- Say *Oh look! There's the monster. What colour is it?* (green) *Is it scary or funny?* (funny) *What's it doing?* (painting)

- Look at all the story pictures (with or without the text on the Image carousel or in the book) on pages 36–39. They guess what happens. Allow suggestions in English or L1.

- Say *Now let's listen to the story.* Say *Let's look at page 36.*

Listening

With books open …

13
- Play the audio or read the story. Learners listen.
- Play the audio or read the story again.

- Pause after page 36 and ask *What's the teacher's name?* (Mr Bath) *What are the children doing?* (reading) *What's the monster painting?* (suns and stars) Teach *star* (draw a star on the board). Say *The monster's painting a star on Anna's …* (shoe)

- Pause after page 37 and say *Now the children are having their …* (lunch) Teach *throw* if necessary. Mime throwing a paper plane and say *The monster's throwing a paper …* (plane) Ask *Can you make paper planes? Is making paper planes fun?* Learners answer.

- Pause after *It's drawing funny faces on the wall* on page 38 and ask *What are the children doing? They're playing …* (sports / soccer, tennis, baseball) Ask *What's the monster doing?* (drawing) *Where's it drawing?* (on the wall) Point to the wall in your classroom. Ask *Can we draw on the walls here?* (no)

- Pause at the end of page 38 and ask *Where are the children going?* (home) *Is the monster going home?* (no) Say *That's right! The monster lives behind the …* (door) *in the children's …* (classroom) Ask one learner to stand and peep out from behind the classroom door.
- At the end of the story, say *The children can see the monster but can the teacher see it?* (no) Point to the last picture and ask *What are they saying?* (goodbye) Say *What's the monster doing? Look! It's playing the …* (piano)

After listening

- Ask *Is the monster happy or sad?* (learners decide) For stronger classes, say *Close your books* and ask *What does the monster do in the story?* (paints suns and stars, throws paper planes, draws funny faces, plays the piano)

 Value

- Point to the first picture and say *The children are reading. Is the monster reading too?* (no) Say *It's …* (painting) Ask *Do we paint on people's shoes?* (no) Say *No, we don't!* Learners repeat.
- Talk about the second picture in the same way: *The children are eating, but what's the monster doing?* (throwing paper planes) Ask *Do you throw paper planes at lunch time?* Encourage learners to answer *No, I don't!*
- Repeat for the picture of the monster drawing on the wall. Then explain in L1 that the monster isn't the same as the children. It behaves differently, but the children still love it. It's a naughty but funny friend. Say *Even when people are very different from us too, we can all be friends.* Explain that diversity (the differences in life) makes things interesting and exciting.
- Ask *Do you like the monster?* (yes) Say *So do I!* Practise this phrase with the whole class.

A Read and write.
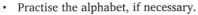
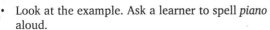

- Practise the alphabet, if necessary.
- Look at the example. Ask a learner to spell *piano* aloud.
- Learners complete the other words in pairs. Check answers in open class or use Presentation plus. Ask different learners to spell the words.

Answers:

2 classmates   **3** tablet   **4** paper   **5** Tennis

Extension:

Learners make their own word puzzles, like the ones in Activity A. They should only choose words they know and can see in the story pictures. If necessary, write words to choose from on the board, e.g. *board, tables, chairs, books, clock, piano, paints, fish, chips, peas, paper planes, juice, bread, playground, baseball bats, ball, bags, door, posters, pens, bee, robot, teacher*. Learners give their word puzzles to a partner to solve.

B Look and read. Choose the correct word.
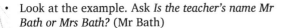

- Look at the example. Ask *Is the teacher's name Mr Bath or Mrs Bath?* (Mr Bath)
- Learners circle the correct words, and then check their answers in pairs. If they can't remember, they can find them in the story.
- Ask different learners to read out the correct sentences.

Answers:

2 jungle   **3** shoe   **4** fish   **5** wall   **6** behind   **7** can't
8 piano

C Read the questions. Listen and write a name or a number.

- Tell learners they are going to listen to a girl talking to her dad. She is talking about the monster. Look at the example questions and answers.

- Learners read the questions. For each question, ask *Is this answer a name or a number?*
- Play the audio. Pause for learners to write. Play it again. Learners compare their answers in pairs.
- Check answers in open class. For the names, ask *How do you spell that?*

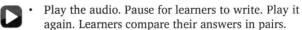
14

Answers:

1 Park (Street)   **2** 10   **3** 17   **4** Kim   **5** 14

Tapescript:

Anna: Hi Dad! I love my friend, the monster!

Dad: What's its name?

Anna: Hobby. You spell that *H-O-B-B-Y*.

Dad: Hobby? That's a funny name.

Anna: The monster can read lots of words now.

Dad: How many letters can the monster read?

Anna: It can read nine words, now. Nine words!

Dad: That's very good.

Can you see the answers? Now you listen and write a name or a number.

1 **Dad:**   Where does Hobby live?

   Anna: It lives at Park Street School.

   Dad: Pardon? At which school?

   Anna: Park Street. You spell that *P-A-R-K*.

2 **Dad:**   Which classroom is Hobby in?

   Anna: It's in classroom 10.

   Dad: In classroom 10? Your classroom?

   Anna: Yes!

3 **Anna:** Hobby loves colouring with its new crayons.

   Dad: How many crayons has it got?

   Anna: Lots and lots. It's got 17.

   Dad: 17! That is a lot!

4	Anna:	Hobby loves eating chips, too!
	Dad:	Does it? Who gives it chips?
	Anna:	Kim. Kim's one of my classmates.
	Dad:	Oh! Do you spell his name *K-I-M*?
	Anna:	Yes. That's right.
5	Anna:	And Hobby has got lots of paints.
	Dad:	Oh! How many?
	Anna:	14. They're in a big box.
	Dad:	14! Fantastic.
	Anna:	Yes. It loves painting on my shoe!
	Dad:	Ha ha!

Test tip: STARTERS
Listening (Part 2)

✔ In Part 2, learners need to write numbers or names. The names are always Starters words but might not come from the list of names. For example, learners might need to write *(Mr) Chips*, *Pear (Tree School)* or *Duck (Street)*. The words are always spelled out.

➔ Give learners plenty of practice hearing and writing the letters of the alphabet. The vowels often cause difficulty, so make sure learners can confidently hear and write *a*, *e*, *i*, *o* and *u*.

Look, read and write.

- Review/Teach the present continuous if necessary. Ask questions about the picture on page 36: *What is Mr Bath doing?* (writing) *What are the children doing?* (reading) *What is the monster doing?* (painting)

- Point to the boy in yellow in the first picture in Activity D. Say *This is Fred. What is he doing?* (drawing) Point to the example answer. Repeat the question for picture 2 and point to the answer (sleeping).

- Learners work in pairs to complete the other sentences with words in the box.

- Check answers in open class.

Answers:

Picture 1: **b** singing, **c** writing, **d** painting
Picture 2: **b** isn't, drinking, **c** writing, eating, **d** painting, reading

Extension:

Prepare 12 pieces of paper with different instructions on them. Fold them up and put them in a hat or bag. One learner chooses an instruction, reads it and gives it back to you. He/She mimes the action. The class guess what the learner is doing. The learner who guesses correctly takes the next instruction.

Suggested actions:
You are eating. You are drinking. You are laughing. You are standing. You are jumping. You are sleeping. You are sitting. You are painting. You are drawing. You are waving. You are reading. You are writing.

Extension: Photocopiable 5

Give each learner a photocopy of '5 Anna's classmates' (TB page 50).
Learners look at the picture. If they know *o'clock* and time, ask *What's the time now?* (11 o'clock) *Is it the morning or the afternoon?* (the morning) Point to one of the computers and ask *What's this?* (a computer) *How many children are there in the classroom?* (eight) *What's the teacher doing?* (drawing)
Ask *Where's Anna?* (learners point) Ask *How do you spell 'Anna'?* (A-double-N-A) *What's Anna doing?* (listening)
Say *Now find Anna's classmates in the picture. Read the sentences and write their names on the picture.*
In pairs, learners read the sentences and write the correct names in the spaces.

Answers:

1 Fred   **3** Lucy   **4** Sue   **5** Tom   **6** Ben   **7** Grace
8 Sam

Extension:

In pairs, learners take turns to ask *How do you spell your name?* and write the name on their partner's sheet.

Read. Choose a word from the box and write.

- Point to the picture on page 37. Ask *What are the children doing?* (having lunch / eating) Say *Yes, they're eating in the …* (dining room) Write *dining room* on the board.

- Look at Activity E. Point to the example.

- Learners read the text first and think about the missing words. They try to guess before they look at the words in the box. Learners then read the text again and use the words in the box to complete the text.

- Check answers in open class or use Presentation plus.

Answers:

1 books   **2** chairs   **3** table   **4** chips   **5** juice

Test tip: STARTERS
Reading and Writing (Part 4)

✔ In Part 4, all the gaps are singular or plural nouns. The words and their picture supports are shown below the text.

➔ Make sure learners can copy words accurately. Remind them that only one word will fit each gap. The word must make sense and also be grammatically correct. Give learners plenty of practice at combining singular and plural nouns with their correct verb forms.

Look and write. Then ask and answer.

- Say *Look. What am I doing? I'm …* Mime listening to music. Learners guess (listening to music). Repeat with more activities (include those in Activity F).

- Point to the first picture, the word box and the example answer. Say *Now you! Write the words under their pictures.* Then they compare answers in pairs.

Answers:

2 listening to music   **3** counting   **4** drawing animals
5 making a poster   **6** painting   **7** spelling long words
8 colouring

What do you like doing?

- Ask *What do you like doing at school?* Ask some learners about the activities in F, e.g. *Do you like reading?* Encourage short form answers (Yes, I do / No, I don't). Say *Me too, So do I* or *Oh, I don't!*

- One learner reads out the first speech bubble. Other learners call out *So do I!* or *Oh, I don't!* Explain, in L1, that when someone says they like (doing) something or they like someone, if we feel the same way, we can say *So do I!* or *Me too!* If we don't feel the same way, we can say *Oh, I don't!* or *Really? I don't!*

- Say *I love playing football!* All the learners who agree with you say *So do I!* All the learners who disagree with you say *Oh, I don't!* Repeat with different statements about what you like doing.

- Learners ask and answer in pairs or small groups.

G Listen and tick (✔) the box.

- Point to the pictures in row 1. Ask *What is the monster playing?* (tennis, hockey, football) Do the same for row 2 (a tablet, paper, crayons).

- Say *Now listen to a boy and a woman. They are talking about the monster. Listen and tick the correct answer. Tick A, B or C.*

15

- Play the audio. Pause after the first dialogue. Give learners time to tick their answer. Play the second dialogue and pause again. Play the audio once or twice more.

- Check answers. Encourage stronger learners to say why the answer is correct, using a complete sentence (e.g. It's playing hockey. There's a tablet in its bag.)

Answers:

1 B   2 A

Tapescript:

See TB pages 55–56

H Look. Ask and answer.

- Point to the picture and say *Look. Where are these monsters?* (in the classroom / in classroom 10) *How many monsters are there?* (five) *What colour are they?* (green, orange, blue, yellow and pink)

- Look at the example question and answer. Ask *What's the orange monster doing?* (It's writing.) Ask about the green, blue and yellow monsters in open class, or learners can ask and answer in pairs.

Answers:

What is the green monster doing? It is playing with a ball / throwing a ball. What is the blue/yellow monster doing? It is drawing (pictures / funny faces).

Extension:

Learners use their imaginations to say more about the five monsters. If necessary, prompt learners with questions, e.g. *Where do these monsters live? What does the orange monster like eating? Can the blue monster play the guitar? What is the green monster saying to the orange monster?*
In groups, learners then find three things to say about the classroom in the picture. Groups take turns to tell the class, e.g. *The walls are yellow. The door is red. The board is green. There are four tables. There is a computer. It is night. There is a moon. There are stars.*

26

> 👍 **Let's say! Page 74**
>
> Say *Look at page 74. Listen.* Play the audio. Say *Let's say* /iː/ *tree.* Learners repeat. Say *Tell me more English words with* /iː/. Learners answer (e.g. see). Repeat with sounds /ɑː/ *guitar* (e.g. class, basketball) /uː/ *balloon* (e.g. blue, shoe).

Let's have fun!

Make a monster and write about it.

Learners look at Activity 5 on page 70. Explain in L1 that they are going to make a monster. Provide a range of materials (card, wool, paper, stickers, plastic bottles, etc.) for learners to use. They can make a monster as on page 70 or a different one using any other different materials, e.g. a finger puppet. Ask *How many (eyes/ears) has your monster got? You choose!*

Learners make, draw or stick on their own choice of details to make a monster. Learners show their monster to other pairs and talk about it using the prompts on page 70, e.g. *Our monster is funny. It's happy too! It likes eating shoes! It lives in the sea.*

Alternatively, learners draw a monster, complete the sentences and then read them out. Display the monsters if possible.

Let's speak!

Talk about a friend. Ask and answer.

Learners look at Activity 5 on page 73. Explain in L1 that learners are going to describe a friend. Review/ Teach positive adjectives *cool, fantastic, great, nice.*

Write some ideas on the board as prompts:

They like playing badminton/basketball/football/ hockey/table tennis/tennis.

(Name) likes painting / playing the piano / reading.

Learners work in pairs and take turns to talk about a friend. After a few minutes, ask different learners about their friend: *Tell me about your friend.* Learners answer.

Home FUN booklet
Pages 16–17 school
Picture dictionary: school

Go online

to practise your English
to listen to the audio recordings
to find more FUN activities!

6 I want that game!

Main topics:	transport
Story summary:	Children in different parts of the city all want the latest computer game, but when they get to the shop there's only one copy left. They all decide to let a younger child have the last game.
Main grammar:	*mine, yours, his, hers, theirs, ours, this/that, these/those*
Main vocabulary:	*Bill, brother, bus, car, computer, computer game, drive, evening, fantastic, father, fly, give, helicopter, keyboard, lorry, motorbike, mouse, phone* (v), *sad, ship, skateboard, smile, store, street, Sue, take, Tom, train, want*
Value:	Being kind (*"Don't worry!"*)
Let's say!:	/ɔː/ /ɜː/ /ə/
Practice tasks:	Speaking Part 4 (D), Speaking Part 2 (Let's speak!)
Test tasks:	Reading and Writing Part 1 (E), Listening Part 3 (F)
Equipment:	

- audio: Story, D, F, I
- (presentation **PLUS**) flashcards

  (206 *computer game*, 214 *helicopter*, 216 *motorbike*, 212 *bus*, 215 *lorry*; 151 *street*, 150 *shop/store*, 73 *father*, 72 *brother*): Storytelling; (21 *mouse – animal*, 161 *mouse – computer*): H; (211 *boat*, 212 *bus*, 213 *car*, 214 *helicopter*, 215 *lorry*, 216 *motorbike*, 217 *plane*, 218 *ship*, 219 *train*, 191 *skateboard*, 186 *kite*): I
- real computer games (optional): Storytelling

- (presentation **PLUS**) Image carousel 45–52

  (8 pictures of modern and old methods of transport): Storytelling, Project
- Photocopy 6 (TB page 51), one per learner (optional): Let's speak!
- large piece of paper, pictures of methods of transport from today and the past, scissors, glue, blank paper, crayons or colouring pens for each group of four or five learners: Let's have fun!

Storytelling

Before listening

With books closed …

- Show a computer game or a flashcard of one and say *This is a computer … (game)* Ask *Who likes playing computer games?* Learners put up their hands. Ask those learners *Which games have you got?* Learners say names.
- Show flashcards or toys for *helicopter, motorbike, bus, lorry.* For each one ask *What's this?* Write the words on the board.
- Mime waiting for a bus, waiting for doors to open, paying the driver, taking a ticket and finding a seat. Ask *What am I in now?* Learners choose an answer from the board. (a bus)
- Use the flashcards to review/teach, if necessary, *street, store, father, brother.* Review/Teach *parents, little girl* and *uncle.*
- Look at the first story picture without the story text on the Image carousel or with the story text in the book on page 44. Ask *Where are the children?* (at home) *What are they doing?* (watching TV) Say *Point to the child on the mat. The child on the floor. The child under the curtain.* (learners point)
- Look at all the story pictures (with or without the text on the Image carousel or in the book) on pages 44–47. On page 45 ask *Where's the helicopter?* (learners point) *What colour is it?* (red) *Where's the motorbike?* (learners point) *What colour is it?* (red) On page 46 ask *Can you see the girl on the bus? Where's the lorry?* (learners point)
- Say *Now let's listen to the story.* Say *Let's look at page 44.*

Listening

With books open …

 Play the audio or read the story. Learners listen.

16 Play the audio or read the story again.

- Pause after page 44 and ask *What are the children's names?* (Tom, Sue, Lucy, Bill) Say *They all want a new … (computer game)*
- Pause after page 45 and ask *Who flies the helicopter? Tom's … (father) Who rides a motorbike? Sue's … (sister)* Say *The children are going to a store. Which store?* (the computer game store)
- Pause after page 46 and ask *Who goes to the store on the bus?* (Lucy) *Who goes in a lorry?* (Bill) Point to the second picture and ask *Where are the children now?* (in the store)
- At the end of the story ask *Have Tom, Sue, Lucy and Bill got the computer game?* (no) *Who's got the computer game?* (the little girl)

After listening

- In L1 if necessary, encourage learners to explain why the little girl has the computer game. Check learners understand *only one game* and *crying*.

 Value

- Look at the first picture on SB page 47 and say *The children want the computer game. They go to the store. How many games are there in the shop?* (one) Point to the little girl in the picture and ask *Who do they see in the shop?* (a little girl) Say *The little girl is sad.* (make a sad face) *She's crying.* (mime crying) Ask *What do the children say?* (Don't cry! Don't worry! Don't be sad!) Check understanding. Ask *Does Bill have the computer game?* (no) *Does he give it to the little girl?* (yes)

- Point to the last picture on SB page 47 and ask *Is the little girl sad now?* (no, happy) *What does she say?* (Thanks!)

- Say *The children want the game. But they give the game to the little girl.*

- In L1, ask *Are you kind/generous? When do you give things to other people? Do you know anyone who is very kind?*

- Stronger learners role play the last part of the story in groups of five (four children and the little girl).

A   Look and write.

- Learners look at the pictures. Ask *Where's the (lorry)?* Learners point.

- Do the example. Ask *How do you spell 'helicopter'?* Learners take turns to say the letters.

- Say *Complete the words.* Learners try to spell the words. They compare answers in pairs.

- Check answers in open class or use Presentation plus.

- In pairs, learners can practise *How do you spell …?* with the five words.

Answers:

2 bus   3 helicopter   4 lorry   5 motorbike

Extension:

Ask about transport: *What colour is your school bus? Has your family got a car? Who drives it? Have you got a bike? What colour is it? Do you go on trains or ride on motorbikes?*

B   Look, read and write.

- Do the example. Different learners read sentences 2–6.

- Learners write the missing words.

- Check answers in open class or use Presentation plus.

Answers:

2 Fun   3 dad/father   4 Candy   5 Lucy   6 Bill

C   Who says this? Draw lines.

- Learners look at the pictures of the children. Ask *Where's Lucy? Where's Bill? Can you see Sue? And Tom?* Learners point. In pairs, learners ask and answer *Who's this? It's Bill.*

- Do the example. Say *Now you! Who says this? Draw lines.* Learners look at the story if necessary to remember and then look back to check their answers.

- Check answers in open class or use Presentation plus.

- Practise pronunciation of *Don't cry! Don't worry!* and *Don't be sad!* Notice that /t/ at the end of *Don't* almost disappears when the next word starts with a consonant. In pairs, learners practise the phrases. Learner A looks sad or mimes crying and Learner B says one of the phrases.

- Ask in L1 *What else can you say to a friend who is scared, unhappy or worried?* (learners' suggestions) *What other things can you do to cheer a friend up and be kind?* (phone them, play a game with them, give them a hug / a present / a cake)

Answers:

2 d   3 c   4 a

D   Write numbers 2–6 in the boxes.

- Use items in the classroom and learners' possessions to review/teach *yours, mine, his, hers, theirs, ours*. Write the words on the board. Use items that belong to boys and girls to practise *his* and *hers*.

- Hold up things and ask *Whose is this? / Whose are these?* Point and ask *Whose is that? / Whose are those?* Learners answer (e.g. It is / They are hers).

- In L1 explain that this is a puzzle. They have to read the conversation to work out the order and find out which two people the game belongs to.

- Learners number the sentences in order. Check answers.

Answers:

2 Sue, 3 Nick, 4 Lucy and Jake, 5 Anna, 6 Tom and Bill
It's Tom and Bill's.

Extension:

Learners work in groups of four. Each learner puts two of his/her possessions on a central desk, e.g. a pen and a notebook. The group looks at all the items and then learners take it in turns to talk about which person one item belongs to, e.g. *This pen is mine. That book is his. That pencil case is yours.* Walk around and ask groups about the items, e.g. *Is this yours? Is this hers?*

E Look and read. Put a tick (✔) or a cross (✗) in the box.

- A learner reads the first example. Ask *Is that right? Yes?* (make a tick gesture) *Or no?* (make a cross gesture) Learners say *Yes*. Repeat for the second example (No).
- Say *Look at the pictures and read. Put a tick or a cross.*
- Learners complete the activity on their own.
- Copy the sentences on the board with the boxes. Learners come to the board to tick or cross each sentence (or use Presentation plus).
- Stronger learners write correct sentences for the wrong answers. (2 This is a train. 5 This is a TV/ television.)

Answers:

1✔ 2✗ 3✔ 4✔ 5✗

Test tip: STARTERS
Reading and Writing (Part 1)

✔ In Part 1, each picture and its sentence will be either singular or plural, e.g. (picture of a ball) *This is a ball* or (picture of two books) *These are books*. The nouns come from a range of topics.
→ Help learners practise this task. Draw objects on the board (singular or plural) and write *This is / These are* sentences under the pictures. Make sentences right or wrong. For wrong sentences, choose another word from the same topic list (e.g. *boat / bus*) or another word that looks similar (e.g. *car / cat*). Learners draw ticks or crosses in the air.

F Listen and tick (✔) the box.

- Read the example question and ask *What can you see in picture A?* (a robot) *And in B?* (a car) *And in C?* (a doll) Play the example. Ask *Which is correct?* (A) Say *Now you! Listen and tick A, B or C.*

 17

- Play the audio. Pause after the first dialogue. Give learners time to tick their answer. Play the second conversation and pause again. Then play the recording once or twice more, if necessary.
- Check answers. In L1, explain the difference between *boat* (small, used for taking one or only a few people on short trips) and *ship* (large, used for taking lots of people or things on long journeys across the sea).

Answers:

1 C   2 A   3 B   4 B   5 A

Tapescript:

Which toy is the baby picking up now?

Girl: What is the baby picking up now, Dad? Her doll?

Man: No. Her robot. She loves it.

Girl: Yes. Where is her toy car?

Man: I don't know. Sorry.

Can you see the tick? Now you listen and tick the box.

---

1   What is Tom drawing?

Woman: Tom's doing some drawing on the computer.

Girl: Fantastic! What is he drawing? An alien?

Woman: No, a ship.

Girl: Great!

2   What is in the box?

Boy: What is in the box, Grandpa? Is it a game?

Man: No, it isn't.

Boy: Your new glasses?

Man: No, it is a phone. But it isn't mine. It's Grandma's.

3   Which is May's favourite store?

Boy: Which is your favourite store, May?

Girl: I love going to the candy store. What is yours?

Boy: I like the games store. Do you?

Girl: It's OK. The bookshop is OK, too.

4   Where is Dad's motorbike?

Girl: Where's Dad's motorbike? It isn't under the tree.

Woman: Is it next to the wall?

Girl: No. Oh! It is there – in the street. Dad is cleaning it.

Woman: Good!

5   Whose tennis racket is it?

Boy: Whose tennis racket is this? Is it yours, Mum?

Woman: No. It is your sister's. It is new.

Boy: Oh. Can Nick play with it?

Woman: No, he can't. Sorry.

Test tip: STARTERS
Listening (Part 3)

✔ In Part 3, learners hear two people talking about an activity, a person or where something is, for example. Learners will hear something about all three pictures but only one picture shows the correct answer. Learners tick the correct picture.
→ Train learners to look at the three pictures carefully before they listen to each conversation and to look for differences between them.

G Look, write and say.

- Learners look at the picture. Ask three or four learners *What can you see?* (bikes, a bus, a lorry, etc.) Explain that in British English, *lorry* or *truck* are now used almost interchangeably. In American English you only hear *truck*.
- Learners work in pairs. Say *Now you! Write a long sentence on the lines.*
- When learners have finished, say *Count your words.* The pair with the most words writes them on the board. Other learners add any different words.

Possible answer:

I can see a boat, some bikes, a motorbike, some cars, a bus, a lorry, a train, a helicopter and a plane.

H Read and draw lines.

- Draw a mouse (the animal) with a long tail on the board or show the flashcard. Draw or show the flashcard of a computer mouse or use the picture in the book. Explain in L1 these have the same name because they look similar and both have long tails!

- Point to the computer in Activity H. Ask *What's this?* Do the same for the keyboard and the skateboard on the screen.

- Do the example. Say *Draw lines from the words to the correct part of the picture.*

- Learners draw lines on their own and compare answers in pairs.

- Check answers in open class.

I Listen and sing the song.

- Show the flashcards for transport (*boat, bus, car, helicopter, lorry, motorbike, plane, ship, train*) and also *skateboard* and *kite*.

- Mime driving/riding on some of the things (e.g. sailing a ship, flying a kite, standing on a skateboard). Ask *What am I driving / riding on / standing on?* etc. Learners answer using words on the board.

18

- Play the first verse of the song. Show the flashcard for *ship*. Ask *Can you fly a ship?* (no!) Point to the next gap and the words on the board. Ask *Which word goes here?* (kite) Learners write *kite* in the space.

- Repeat for all the verses of the song, so that at the end learners have completed the song.

- Play the song a second time. Learners join in.

- Divide the class into groups A and B to sing the song. Group A asks the questions. Group B answers. Repeat. Group B asks and group A answers.

28

- You can also listen to a version of this song without the words for learners to sing along to.

Answers:

1 kite **2** motorbike **3** truck **4** skateboard

Tapescript:

See TB page 58

Extension:

Write *fly, drive, ride* in a cloud on the board. Write the following words in another cloud: *skateboard, kite, horse, bus, lorry, plane, motorbike, helicopter, train.* Learners work in pairs to match verbs with nouns. Set a time limit of two minutes.
Check answers in open class.

Answers:

fly a kite, fly a plane, fly a helicopter; drive a bus, drive a lorry, drive a train; ride a skateboard, ride a horse, ride a motorbike

---

26

Let's say! **Page 74**

Say *Look at page 74. Listen.* Play the audio. Say *Let's say* /ɔː/ st**o**ry. Learners repeat. Say *Tell me more English words with* /ɔː/. Learners answer (e.g. door). Repeat with sounds /ɜː/ b**ir**d (e.g. shirt, hers) and /ə/ monst**er** (e.g. a, father).

---

6 Let's have fun!

Make a transport poster.

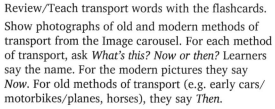

Review/Teach transport words with the flashcards.

Show photographs of old and modern methods of transport from the Image carousel. For each method of transport, ask *What's this? Now or then?* Learners say the name. For the modern pictures they say *Now.* For old methods of transport (e.g. early cars/motorbikes/planes, horses), they say *Then.*

Divide the class into groups of four or five. Give each group a large piece of paper (poster size). Show learners how to draw a vertical line on the paper to make two sections, like the one on Student's Book page 70. Write *Then* and *Now* on the board. Learners copy *Then* above the left-hand section on their poster and *Now* on the right.

Learners cut out and glue or tape pictures in the correct section of their poster (old cars, bikes, buses, etc. under *Then*, and modern cars, planes, trains, etc. under *Now*).

Learners label the photos, according to their ability, e.g. *This is an old bus. / My grandfather loves this old bus. This is a new car. / You can drive this car now.*

Display the posters around the classroom.

6 Let's speak!

What is this? Ask and answer.

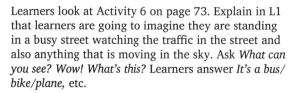

Learners look at Activity 6 on page 73. Explain in L1 that learners are going to imagine they are standing in a busy street watching the traffic in the street and also anything that is moving in the sky. Ask *What can you see? Wow! What's this?* Learners answer *It's a bus/bike/plane,* etc.

Give each pair of learners a photocopy of '6 Transport' (TB page 51). Ask two learners to read out the speech bubbles: *What's this? It's a bus.* Learners work in pairs and ask and answer questions about the picture.

Two learners read out the speech bubbles about travelling to school. Ask *How do you come to school? On a bus? In a car? On your bike? In a train? Draw and write.* Learners draw a picture of them travelling to school and complete the sentence.

Display their pictures on the classroom wall if possible.

Home FUN booklet
Pages 20–21, 22–23 toys, transport
Picture dictionary: transport

Go online

to practise your English
to listen to the audio recordings
to find more FUN activities!

Monkey beach

7

Main topics:	leisure
Story summary:	Eva is relaxing on the beach and, as people stop to talk to her, a naughty monkey starts taking her things. When she finally sees the monkey, she laughs and makes friends with it.
Main grammar:	*have* + noun + *to* ... (e.g. *She has some juice to drink.*), present continuous
Main vocabulary:	*alien, bat* (n), *behind, burger, clap* (v), *coconut, egg, enjoy, Eva, face, grapes, guitar, have fun, hit, juice, kiwi, lemonade, lime, mangoes, monkey, pencil, racket, rice, sand, sing, sofa, table, take photos, tomato, water, wave* (v)
Value:	Being happy (*"Be happy!"*)
Let's say!:	/θ/ /ð/
Practice tasks:	Speaking Part 4 (C), Speaking Part 2 (E)
Test tasks:	Listening Part 1 (E), Reading and Writing Part 3 (F), Speaking Part 1 (H)

Equipment:	• ▶ audio: Story, E
	• flashcards
	(220 *sand*, 98 *lime*, 95 *kiwi*, 99 *mango*, 89 *coconut*): Storytelling; (43 *baseball cap*, 49 *jacket*, 57 *T-shirt*, 46 *glasses*, 44 *boots*, 80 *banana*, 83 *burger*, 105 *pear*, 107 *pineapple*, 176 *bike*, 182 *guitar*, 94 *juice*, 101 *milk*): D Extension; (83 *burger*, 90 *egg*, 92 *grapes*, 97 *lemonade*, 112 *tomato*, 109 *rice*): F

• presentation **PLUS** Image carousel 53–60 (3 pictures of happy people): C, (5 pictures of different types of monkeys): Let's have fun!
• real beach bag with items (e.g. sunglasses, a kiwi, orange juice, a book, a hat): Let's speak!
• Photocopy 7 (TB page 52), one per learner: Let's speak!
• large piece of paper, pictures of different types of monkeys, scissors, glue, blank paper, for each group of four or five learners: Let's have fun!

⭐ Storytelling

Before listening

With books closed ...

• Show the flashcard *sand* and review/teach the word. Say *We find sand at the ...* (beach) Say *This story is about a girl at the beach.* Ask *Do you like going to the beach?* Learners answer.

• Show flashcards of the fruit in the story (lime, kiwi, mango, coconut). Write the words on the board. Point and ask some learners *Do you like mangoes/kiwis?*

• Say *I'm on the beach. Oh! I can see a friend.* Mime waving and smiling. Say *Hi! How are you?* Say *Now you!* Learners wave and smile saying *Hi! How are you?*

• Look at the first story picture without the story text on the Image carousel or with the story text in the book on page 52. Ask *Where's the girl?* (on the beach) *What can you see?* (e.g. some trees, a guitar, a tablet, a shell, some juice) Ask *Can the girl see the monkey?* (no)

• Look at all the story pictures (with or without the text on the Image carousel or in the book) on pages 52–55. Ask *What does the girl do on the beach?* (plays the guitar, takes photos, talks to friends, sings a song)

• Say *Now let's listen to the story.* Say *Let's look at page 52.*

Listening

With books open ...

Play the audio or read the story. Learners listen.

Play the audio or read the story again.

19

• Pause after page 52 and ask *What's the girl's name?* (Eva) *What's the name of the beach?* (Monkey Beach) *What can Eva drink/eat?* (lime juice, kiwi, mangoes)

• Pause after Eva says, '*Goodbye, Miss Board*' on page 53 and ask *What's the woman's name? Miss ...* (Board) *Can she see the monkey?* (yes) *Can Eva see the monkey?* (no) Play the audio for the rest of page 53 and ask *What's the man's name? Mr ...* (Page) *Can he see the monkey?* (yes) *Can Eva see the monkey?* (no)

• Pause halfway through page 54 and ask *What's the woman's name?* (Mrs Short) Ask *Is the monkey Eva's pet?* (no)

• Pause after page 54 and ask *What's Eva looking for?* (her tablet) *Where is it?* (the monkey has got it)

• At the end of the story ask *Is Eva angry with the monkey?* (no) Say *That's right. She laughs. Let's laugh, too!* Learners laugh with you.

After listening

- Read Eva's speech bubble in the last picture. Ask learners to say what kind of person Eva is in L1. (happy, generous, positive)

 Value

- Look at SB page 53 and say *Miss Board asks Eva 'Are you having fun?'* Ask *Is Eva having fun?* (Yes, she is.) *Mr Page says 'You've got a very happy smile on your face.'* Ask *Is Eva a happy person?* (yes) Say *Now you! Show your happy faces!*
- Look at SB page 54 and say *Mrs Short asks 'How are you?'* *What does Eva say?* (Really great, thank you!) Divide the class into groups A and B. Groups take turns at greeting and responding. Then learners practise in pairs.

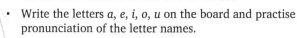

A Look and write. Then draw lines.

- Write the letters *a, e, i, o, u* on the board and practise pronunciation of the letter names.
- Learners look at the picture. Do the example. Say *Now you! Write the letters.* Learners write the missing letters.
- Check answers in open class or use Presentation plus.
- Learners draw lines between the completed words and the items in the picture.
- Ask *How many fruits can you see?* (four) *Which fruit do you like eating? What colour's the sand?* (yellow)

Answers:

coconut   mango   sand   lime

Extension:

Write *lime* on the board and say *lime*, stressing the vowel sound. Underline the *i* and the *e*. Say *Look at the letters. Which words are like this one?* In pairs, learners use their word lists to find more *_i_e* words, e.g. *kite, like, rice, ride, nice, bike.* Say *I ride my nice bike and like eating limes and rice.* Learners repeat.

B Look and read. Choose the correct word.

- Say *Choose the correct word.* Do the example.
- Learners work in pairs to circle the words. Check answers.
- Read sentence 6. Learners repeat it. Clap your hands, point to the learners and say *Clap your hands, too!* Learners copy. You could ask in L1 when learners clap their hands.

Answers:

2 tablet   **3** behind   **4** beautiful   **5** coconut   **6** claps

C Listen and sing the song.

- Mime playing the guitar and ask *What am I doing?* (playing the guitar) Say *Eva plays the guitar on the beach and she sings a …* (song)
- Ask *Do you go to a beach?* (If learners answer *no*, ask *Where do you go? To a park?*) *Who goes with you? What do you do there?*
- Play the audio. Learners listen and follow in their books. Teach actions for *clap your hands, be happy* (thumbs up), *jump* and *smile* (lift hands to face and smile).
- Play the song again. Learners listen and do the actions with you.
- The class could sing this song to start future lessons.
- You can also listen to a version of this song without the words for learners to sing along to.

20

29

D Look and write.

- Model the structure *have + object + infinitive.* Hold up a book and say *I have a new book to read.*
- Learners work in pairs to write the sentences.
- Check answers in open class or using Presentation plus.

Answers:

1 Miss Board has a funny book to read.
2 Mr Page has a new game to play.
3 Mrs Short has an old hat to wear.

Extension:

Show a flashcard and make a sentence with *I have* + noun + verb, e.g. *I have a … (burger) to … (eat).* Repeat with different words, e.g. *I have some … (boots) to … (wear). I have a … (guitar) to … (play). I have some … (milk) to … (drink).*
Possible flashcards to use: *baseball cap, jacket, T-shirt, glasses, boots, banana, burger, pear, pineapple, bike, guitar, juice, milk.* Make sure you don't use nouns which require prepositions after the verb in these sentences (e.g. *I have a radio to listen to. I have a camera to take photos with.*)
When learners are familiar with the language, show flashcards and ask some learners to say the sentences.

E Listen and draw lines.

- In open class, ask questions about the picture. Say *Listen and point. Who's wearing a baseball cap? Who's kicking a ball? Who's playing the guitar? Who's closing the car door? Who's jumping in the sea?* When learners point, ask *Is that a boy or a girl?*
- Play the audio and pause after the example. Ask *Who's the boy? What's his name?* (Hugo) *What's he doing?* (kicking a ball) *Can you see the line from his name?*

21

- Say *Now you! Draw lines from the people to their names.* Learners listen to the rest of the audio. Play the audio a second time. Learners check their answers. If necessary, play the audio again.
- Check answers in open class or with Presentation plus.

Answers:

girl closing the car door – Alice,   boy in the sea – Matt, boy in the red jacket and white jeans – Dan,   girl with the tablet and book – Lucy,   girl with the bag and shells – Jill

Tapescript:

Woman: Hi! Is this Eva's favourite beach?

Boy: Yes. She isn't here, but I know a lot of these people.

Woman: Who's that boy, then? He's kicking the ball.

Boy: That's Hugo. Hugo loves football!

Woman: So do I!

Can you see the line? This is an example.

Now you listen and draw lines.

1 Boy: One of the girls is closing the car door. Can you see her?

Woman: Yes, I can. What's her name?

Boy: That's Alice.

Woman: Can Alice drive that car?

Boy: No! Ha ha!

2 Woman: And who's that boy?

Boy: Oh, that's Matt. He's jumping in the sea!

Woman: Does Matt like swimming in the sea?

Boy: Yes, he loves it.

3 Boy: And look! There's Dan.

Woman: Which boy is he?

Boy: The boy in the red jacket.

Woman: Oh … and white jeans. That's Dan?

Boy: Yes.

4 Woman: Who's that girl? She's got a tablet. Oh, and a book to read.

Boy: Her name's Lucy.

Woman: Lucy?

Boy: Yes! She likes reading about animals.

Woman: Great!

5 Boy: And there's Jill.

Woman: Jill? Which child is she?

Boy: The one with the shells. She's got 20 shells in that bag!

Woman: Wow! Well, thank you for showing me this picture.

Boy: That's OK.

Test tip: STARTERS
Listening (Part 1)

✔ In Part 1, learners hear two people talking about different people in the big picture. Learners must draw lines between five of the people and their correct names. Learners hear information about these five people, e.g. what they are doing, where they are, or what they're wearing or holding.

➜ Make sure learners know that one name will not be used. To help them do this task, learners should understand all the colours, clothes and action verbs on the Starters word list.

Extension:

Use the picture in Activity E to practise Speaking Part 2. Ask questions, e.g. *What's this?* (a boat) *What colour is it?* (blue and white) *How many trees are there?* (four) *What's this boy doing?* (playing the guitar) *Tell me about this beach.* (e.g. It's big. It's nice. I can see a boat. There are lots of children. It's sunny.)

F Look at the pictures. Look at the letters. Write the words.

- Practise the alphabet with books closed.
- If possible, show flashcards *burger, egg, grapes, lemonade, tomato, rice.* Say, e.g. *Point to the tomato* or ask *What's this?* If you don't have flashcards, use the pictures in Activity F.
- Do the example. Point to the first picture and ask *What's this? It's an …* (egg) Point to the jumbled letters and explain in L1 that learners need to put them in the right order. Point to the answer and say *Look, e-g-g. Is that right? Yes. Egg is e-g-g.* Ask *How do you spell 'egg'?* Learners say the letters as a whole class: *e-g-g.*
- Learners do the activity in pairs.
- Check answers in open class or use Presentation plus.
- For each word, ask, e.g. *How do you spell (rice)?* Learners say the letters as a whole class. They count the dashes and count the letters in their word to make sure they have used all the letters.

Answers:

2 rice **3** grapes **4** burger **5** tomato **6** lemonade

G Listen and number the pictures.

- Learners look at the pictures. Point and ask *What are these places?* (a park, a fruit shop, a bookshop, a beach) Say *Listen to Eva now. She's talking to people in these places. Where is she?*
- Play the audio. Pause after the example and point to the number *1.* Say *Now you! Write the number in the box.*

22

- Play the rest of the audio. Learners listen and write numbers *2* to *4.* They compare answers in pairs. Play the audio again if necessary.
- Check answers.

Answers:

1 d **2** b **3** a **4** c

Tapescript:

1 Eva: Good morning! Don't sit in the sun! Come and swim with me.

2 Eva: Good afternoon! I'd like a pineapple and two lemons, please.

3 Eva: Good evening, Mr Short! I love walking here. Do you?

4 Eva: Thank you for this story book. It's really cool! Good night!

H Listen to your teacher and point. Then draw lines.

- Learners look at the big picture. Ask questions and learners point: *Where's the sun? Where are the children? Where's the sea? Where are the boats? Where's the sand? Where are the trees? Where's the table? Where are the elephants?*

- Learners then look at the small object pictures. Ask questions and learners point: *Which is the pencil / sofa / water / alien / train / tennis racket?*

- In the test, the child needs to pick up an object card (not just point to it) and place it on the large picture. To practise for this, learners can draw a line from the small pictures to the correct part of the large picture.

- Say *Which is the water? Put the water on the table.* Show learners how to draw a line.

- Then say *Which is the sofa? Put the sofa next to the elephants.* Learners listen and draw a line.

- Continue asking *Which is …?* questions and give instructions with different prepositions. Ask general questions too, e.g. *How many people can you see?* (four) *How many trees are there?* (five) *Is it afternoon or evening?* (evening)

I Write and say.

- Read the complete sentence. Emphasise the 's' sounds. Ask *How many words start with 's' here?* (eight) Point out that the sentence begins with a name starting with 'S'.

- In pairs or small groups, learners think of ways to complete the other sentences using lots of words that start with 'e', 'd' and 'l'. Help with new vocabulary.

- Pairs/Groups read out one of their funny sentences. They can illustrate their sentence for homework.

Suggested answers:

Eva's enjoying her English story and eating eggs this evening.
Dan's drawing a duck and a dog on his desk and drinking lemonade.
Lucy's learning lots of long words and listening to music in the living room.

Let's have fun!

Make a monkey poster.

Show photographs of different species of monkey from the Image carousel. Ask *Where do monkeys live? What do they eat? What colour are they? How many legs have they got?* Point to a tail and ask *What's this?*

Divide the class into groups of four or five. Learners find out about monkeys, e.g. where they live, what they eat and how they all help each other in their families. Give each group a large piece of paper (poster size). They cut out, draw or print pictures and write about the monkeys. Each group could find out about a different type of monkey (e.g. chimpanzees, marmosets, orang-utans, lemurs).

Display the posters if possible.

Let's speak!

What is in your beach bag? Ask and answer.

Learners look at Activity 7 on page 73. Explain in L1 that learners are going to imagine what is inside a beach bag. Show learners a real beach bag or draw one on the board. Ask *What is in our beach bag? Let's look!* Learners guess what is inside the bag, e.g. *a camera, some lemonade.* Say *Yes! / That's right! / Well done!*

Give each pair of learners a photocopy of '7 What's in your beach bag?' (TB page 52). Learners cut out the nine cards and write the words under each picture (a watermelon, a clock, some flowers, a hat/cap, boots, a phone, a baseball bat and ball, a computer/laptop, a banana).

In pairs, learners take turns to pick up a card and practise saying *Let's take (a watermelon)* and answering *Good idea! / OK!* or *That's silly! / No, not that!* After a few minutes, ask *So, what's in your beach bag?* Learners answer.

Winners!

8

Main topics:	sport
Story summary:	Rival basketball teams play a game. Each child has their part to play to help their team win.
Main grammar:	Question words: *What colour …? How many …? Which …? Where …? Who …? Whose …?, Have you got …?*
Main vocabulary:	*Alex, Alice, bounce, catch, cool, Dan, fast, game, Jill, Jim, Kim, net, Sam, star, start, stop, sun, tall, team, today, Tom, watch* (v), *Well done!, winners*
Value:	Working as a team (*"I'm good at …"*)
Let's say!:	/ɪə/ /eə/
Practice tasks:	Speaking Part 4 (C)
Test tasks:	Reading and Writing Part 2 (D), Reading and Writing Part 5 (E), Listening Part 4 (F), Listening Part 3 (H)

Equipment:	• ▶ audio: Story, F, G • (presentation **PLUS**) flashcards (171 *badminton*, 172 *baseball*, 173 *basketball*, 181 *football/soccer*, 183 *hockey*, 192 *skateboarding*, 194 *table tennis*, 195 *tennis*): Storytelling; (177 *bounce*, 197 *throw*, 178 *catch*, 189 *run*, 193 *swim*, 184 *jump*, 198 *walk*): A Extension • balls for playing different sports (basketball, football, hockey ball, tennis ball, baseball) (optional): Storytelling	• (presentation **PLUS**) Image carousel 61–69 (9 pictures of sports teams and winning competitors): Storytelling • ball: A • crayons or colouring pens: F • soft balls, one per group of five learners: Let's have fun! • Photocopy 8 (TB page 53), one per learner and two extra copies: Let's speak!

Storytelling

Before listening

With books closed …

- Ask *What's your favourite sport?* Write suggestions on the board. Use flashcards or photos to review/teach the Starters sports (badminton, baseball, basketball, football/soccer, hockey, skateboarding, table tennis and tennis).

- Show balls used for different sports and ask *Which sport is this for?* (e.g. tennis) Throw and catch a ball and say *I'm throwing and catching.* Say *Now you!* Three or four learners throw a soft ball to each other. The class says *He's/She's throwing/catching.* Review/Teach *bounce.*

- Show pictures of sports teams from the Image carousel. Say *This is a team. How many teams play in a football game?* (two) *And how many players are there in one football/basketball/hockey team?* (eleven/five/eleven)

- Write 2–1 on the board. Point and say *Look at this score. Team A has two points* (look happy), *but team B only has … (one)* (look sad) *Team A are the winners!* Show photographs of winning teams and athletes from the Image carousel. Say *They're the winners! / He's/She's the winner!*

- Look at the first story picture without the story text on the Image carousel or with the story text in the book on page 60. Ask *How many children can you see?* (five) *How many boys?* (three) *How many girls?* (two) *Which sport are they playing?* (basketball)

- Look at all the story pictures (with or without the text on the Image carousel or in the book) on pages 60–63. In L1, ask them to guess what happens.

- Say *Now let's listen to the story.* Say *Let's look at page 60.*

Listening

With books open …

▶ Play the audio or read the story. Learners listen.

23 Play the audio or read the story again.

- Pause after page 60, point to the boy with red hair and say *This is Alex. What are his friends' names?* (Jill, Kim, Jim, Tom) *Which are girls' names?* (Jill, Kim) *Which are boys' names?* (Jim, Tom) Ask *What's the name of their team?* (the Five Stars) Draw five stars on the board.

- Pause halfway through page 61, point and ask *What's this team's name?* (the Five Suns) *What are these players' names?* (Alice, Dan, Sam, Matt, Pat) *What colour are the Five Stars' T-shirts?* (blue) *What colour are the Five Suns' T-shirts?* (orange)

- Pause after page 61 and say *Look at the score! How many points have the Five Stars got?* (three) *And the Five Suns?* (four) *Who are the winners now?* (the Five Suns)

- Pause after page 62 and ask *Who puts the ball in the net?* (Alex) *Which numbers can you see on the T-shirts?* (four, five, ten)
- At the end of the story ask *What's the score?* (5–4) *Who are the winners?* (the Five Stars) Say *Let's say 'Hooray! Well done, Five Stars!'* Learners repeat.

After listening
- In L1, learners tell the story (the Five Stars were losing, but they won the game in the end). Ask *Which team would you like to play for in the story?*

☆ **Value**
- Ask *Are the Five Stars happy or sad at the end of the game?* (happy) *Are they a good team?* (yes) In L1 discuss why the Five Stars are a good team. *Is it because they are all good at doing different things?* Ask *What's Alex good at?* (throwing) *And who's good at catching?* (Kim and Jim) *And Jill can run …* (very fast)
- In L1, discuss the fact that everyone is good at something and not so good at other things and that's OK because we are all different. But we all have something to be proud about. Explain that in every kind of team (sports/work/family) we need people with different talents.
- Ask *Do you play in a team? What sport do you play? How many children are in the team?*

  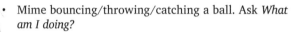

A Look, read and write.

- Mime bouncing/throwing/catching a ball. Ask *What am I doing?*
- Ask two learners to come to the front of the class. Say, e.g. *Start! You are running. You are jumping. You are throwing a ball. You are bouncing a ball on the floor. Stop!* The learners do the actions and then stop.
- Learners open their books.
- Do the example. Point to the other words in the box and say *Now you. Choose and write the correct words.*
- Check answers in open class or use Presentation plus.

Answers:

2 starting   **3** catching   **4** bouncing   **5** smiling

Extension:

Play a mime game with flashcards (*bounce, throw, catch, run, swim, jump, run, walk*). Put the flashcards in a pile at the front of the class. A learner chooses one of the cards, looks at it but keeps it secret. Then he/she mimes the action. Ask *What's he/she doing?* Learners guess (e.g. *He's swimming*). The learner who guesses correctly has the next turn.

B Look, read and write.

- Look at the example in open class.
- In pairs, learners read questions 2–6 and write the answers.
- Check answers in open class or use Presentation plus.

Answers:

2 basketball   **3** the Five Suns   **4** Matt and Pat
5 Alice, Dan and Sam   **6** 5–4

C Who is good at this? Put a tick (✔) in the box.

- Ask *What are players doing in the pictures?* (catching, bouncing, jumping, throwing a ball, running) Point to each word.
- Say each word. Learners mime.
- Do the example in open class.

- Learners re-read the story and complete the table by ticking the actions that the five players are good at. They should do this in pairs. Pairs then check answers with other pairs.
- Check answers in open class or on Presentation plus.
- Ask questions about the completed table, e.g. *Who can't catch the ball, but is very good at throwing?* (Alex) *Who can't throw or jump, but can run very fast?* (Jill) *Which two children are very good at catching?* (Kim and Jim) *Who is good at bouncing, catching, throwing, jumping and running?* (Tom)

Answers:

Learners tick:
Alex: throwing
Jill: running
Kim: catching
Jim: catching
Tom: catching, bouncing, jumping, throwing, running

- Note that *be good at* is a Movers structure but make sure learners understand and can use it here.
- Ask *What do you like doing?* Learners answer. Write suggestions on the board. Learners can help with spellings, e.g. *drawing, singing, taking photos, riding a bike.* Accept nouns too, e.g. *basketball, hockey, table tennis.*
- Point to the words and ask three or four learners *What are you good at?*

Extension:

Stronger learners write sentences about what they are good at.

D Look and read. Write *yes* or *no*.

- Learners look at the picture and read the examples. Say *Count the children. Are there five?* (yes) *And is the kite red and yellow?* (no)
- Learners read the sentences and write *yes* or *no*.
- Check answers in open class or use Presentation plus. Stronger learners can correct the false sentences.

Answers:

1 no   **2** no   **3** yes   **4** no   **5** yes

Extension:

Use the picture for some creative thinking and practice for Speaking Part 3. In groups of three or four, learners think of sentences to answer the following questions:
1 Tell me about the dog.
2 Tell me about the boy with the kite.
3 Tell me about this playground.
Walk around and help learners with vocabulary and structures, if necessary.

Suggested answers:

1 The dog is four years old. That ball is its favourite toy. It's got white legs. 2 The boy is eight years old. He's got a yellow cap. He's good at running. 3 The playground is big. The children like it. You can play basketball there.

E Look at the pictures and read the questions. Write one-word answers.

- Learners look at the first picture in Activity E. Ask *What colour is the bike?* (purple) *And the car?* (red)
- Do the examples in open class.
- Learners read the questions and write their answers in pencil. They compare answers in pairs.
- Check answers in open class or use Presentation plus.

Answers:

1 car   **2** girl   **3** three/3   **4** chair   **5** jumping

F Listen and colour.

- Ask about colours of things in the classroom, e.g. *Point to something (black). Where's a (yellow) thing?*
- Learners look at the picture on Presentation plus or in their books. Ask *Where's the chair? One girl is holding a ball. Which girl is that? Where are the shoes? Where are the doors?* (learners point)

24

- Play the audio. Pause after the first colouring instruction. Ask *Where's the ball?* (on the chair) *What colour is the ball?* (red) Draw a ball on the board and just colour a part of it. Point and say *This colouring is OK!* Explain in L1 that it is enough for this activity but they can finish the colouring at the end of the activity or at home.
- Make sure all learners have crayons or colouring pens including blue, brown, green, pink, purple and red.

- Play the rest of the audio. Learners listen and colour. Play the audio a second time if necessary.
- Check answers in open class or use Presentation plus.
- Stronger learners ask and answer in pairs, e.g. *What colour is the ball under the boy's foot?* (blue)

Answers:

Learners colour the picture: ball that the girl with long black hair is holding – green, ball under the boy's foot – blue, ball between the shoes – brown, ball in girl's bag – pink, ball in front of the door – purple

Tapescript:

Man: What a great picture! Let's colour some of these balls.

Girl: OK. There's a ball on the chair. Can I colour that one?

Man: The ball on the chair? Yes. Colour it red, please.

Girl: OK. There!

Man: Thank you.

Can you see the red ball? This is an example. Now you listen and colour.

1 **Girl:** One girl is holding a ball.

 Man: The girl with the long, black hair?

 Girl: That's right. Can I colour her ball green?

 Man: Yes, you can.

 Girl: Great!

2 **Girl:** And there's a ball under one boy's foot. Look!

 Man: Oh yes! Colour that ball blue, please.

 Girl: The ball under the boy's foot. OK. There!

 Man: Very good.

3 **Man:** One of the balls is between those two shoes.

 Girl: Oh, I can see it. Can I colour that ball brown?

 Man: Yes!

 Girl: OK. I'm colouring the ball between the shoes now, too.

4 **Man:** Now colour the ball in the bag.

 Girl: The ball in the bag?

 Man: Yes. Colour it pink. Have you got that colour?

 Girl: Yes, I have. I'm colouring it now.

 Man: Fantastic.

5 **Man:** Now find the ball in front of the door.

 Girl: I can see it.

 Man: Good. Colour the ball in front of the door …

 Girl: Purple?

 Man: OK! Yes!

 Girl: That's my favourite colour!

 Man: It's mine too! Good. Well done!

G Read and draw lines.

- Learners look at the example line. Point to the first blue speech bubble and say *One of the Five Stars asks this question.* Point to the matching purple speech bubble and say *One of the Five Suns answers it.*
- Learners match each blue speech bubble with a purple one.
- Check answers in open class or on Presentation plus.

Listen and tick (✔) the box.

- Read the question and point to each picture in the example. Ask *What is Alex doing here? And here? And here?* (drinking, reading, throwing a ball) Play the example. Ask *Tick A, B or C?* (B) Tick box B as an example.

- Tell learners they are going to listen to three more conversations. There are two people talking in each conversation.

- Say *Now you! Listen to the people and tick A, B or C.*

25

- Play the audio. Learners tick their answers. Play the audio again for learners to check their answers and a third time if necessary.

- Check answers in open class.

Answers:

1 B   2 A   3 C   4 A

Tapescript:

See TB pages 55–56

Test tip: STARTERS
Listening (Part 3)

✔ Something about all three pictures will be mentioned in each conversation. However, only one picture will be correct. The information learners hear for the correct answer might come at the beginning, in the middle or at the end of the conversation.

→ Train learners to listen very carefully to the whole of each conversation.

- To conclude, say *Let's talk about sport and games!* Ask some learners *What's your favourite sport? Where do you play games? Who do you play with?* Learners can also ask and answer the questions in pairs.

- Finally, say *Well done! This is the end of your book! You can say 'Hooray!'*

Let's say! Page 74

26

Say *Look at page 74. Listen.* Play the audio. Say *Let's say* /ɪə/ **ear.** Learners repeat. Say *Tell me more English words with* /ɪə/. Learners answer (e.g. here). Repeat with sound /eə/ **chair** (e.g. bear, where).

Let's have fun!

Let's throw and catch the ball. Play a game.

Play the following game outside if possible. Divide learners into teams of five. Learners stand in small circles. Tell each learner what team number they are, e.g. *You're number one/two/three/four/five.*

Give each team's 'number one' player a soft ball. Give clear, loud instructions, e.g.

Number one! Throw the ball to number two!

Number two! Catch the ball and throw it to number three.

Number three! Catch the ball and bounce it to number four!

Number four! Catch the ball and jump! Now throw the ball to number five!

Number five! Catch the ball, but don't throw it! Run to me and give me the ball.

Let's speak!

Tick (✔) the sports you can do. Find a partner.

Ask learners to turn to page 73 in their Student's Book and look at Activity 8.

Give each learner a photocopy of '8 Which sports can you do?' (TB page 53).

Prepare two extra copies with two ticks next to the same pictures (e.g. swimming and baseball ticked on both pages). Leave the other tick boxes empty.

Point to each picture and ask *Which sport is this? And this?* etc. (table tennis, swimming, badminton, hockey, baseball, horse riding) Point to the table tennis picture and then to the tick box and say *I can play table tennis. Tick the box.*

In pairs, learners take turns to ask and answer about the sports: *Can you …? Yes, I can. / No, I can't.*

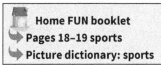

Home FUN booklet
Pages 18–19 sports
Picture dictionary: sports

Go online

to practise your English
to listen to the audio recordings
to find more FUN activities!

The home

1 Look, read and circle.

1 There's a (bathroom) / **dining room** in the house.
2 There's a **picture** / **mirror** in the bedroom.
3 There's a **table** / **rug** in the living room.
4 There's a **desk** / **box** in the bedroom.
5 There are some **cats** / **flowers** in the kitchen.
6 There's a **bookcase** / **cupboard** in the living room.

2 Look and count. Complete the sentences.

1 There are 12 .... ducks.
2 .... balloons.
3 .... frogs.
4 .... snakes.
5 .... hats.
6 .... oranges.

What's your favourite animal?

2

Draw, read and write.

My favourite animal is ....

How many legs has it got?	My animal has got .... legs.
What colour is your animal?	My animal is ....
What can your animal do? Can it swim? Fly? Run?	My animal can ....
What does it like eating?	My animal likes eating ....
Is your animal big or small, ugly or beautiful?	My animal is ....

3 # We like ...

Look and write.

....

....

....

....

....

....

....

....

....

My name is

....

I like

....

My favourite food

Anna's classmates

What are the classmates' names?

~~Anna~~ Fred Sam Lucy Tom Sue Grace Ben

2 ....Anna.......

1 ....

4 ....

7 ....

6 ....

3 ....

8 ....

5 ....

Anna and Fred are listening to a song on one of the computers.

Ben and Tom are drawing on one of the computers. Tom is smiling.

Sam and Grace are playing a game on the computer. Grace has got black hair.

Sue and Lucy are writing on one of the computers. Sue has got long hair.

Her classmate Lucy has got short hair.

My name is ....

Transport

What's this? Ask and answer.

What's this?

It's a bus.

Do you go to school on a bus?

No, I don't.

Now draw and write.

I go to school ....

What's in your beach bag?

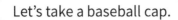

Let's take a baseball cap.

Good idea!

Let's take some watermelon.

No that's silly!

Which sports can you do?

Which sports can you do? Tick (✓) the box.

STORYFUN ②

To: ....

Name of school: ....

Date: ....

Signed: ....

Well done!

Extra tapescripts

12

Unit 4 Activity H

Girl:	Hello! Look at this photo of my cousin.
Woman:	Wow! It's great. What's his name?
Girl:	His name is Mark.
Woman:	Mark?
Girl:	Yes. You spell that *M-A-R-K*.
Woman:	How old is he?
Girl:	He's 12 years old.
Woman:	12?
Girl:	Yes, that's right.

Can you see the answers? Now you listen and write a name or number.

1   Woman: Where does Mark live?
     Girl: He lives next to Mr Gray.
     Woman: Cool!
     Girl: The name of that street is Show Street.
     Woman: Show Street? Do you spell that *S-H-O-W*?
     Girl: Yes. It's nice there.

2   Girl: Mark's got a dog.
     Woman: Oh! What's his dog's name?
     Girl: His dog's name is Teddy!
     Woman: Teddy! What a great name! Do you spell that *T-E-D-D-Y*?
     Girl: Yes! Mark really loves his dog.

3   Girl: Mark loves Mr Gray's chickens, too.
     Woman: That's nice. How many chickens has Mr Gray got?
     Girl: He's got 16 chickens.
     Woman: 16! That's a lot!
     Girl: Yes! Mark likes counting their eggs!

4   Girl: Mark likes the cows, too.
     Woman: What's the name of his favourite cow?
     Girl: Its name is Fun! *F-U-N*!
     Woman: 'Fun' is a very funny name for a cow!
     Girl: Ha ha! Yes, it is.

5   Girl: And Mark likes giving food to Mr Gray's goats.
     Woman: How many goats has Mr Gray got?
     Girl: He's got eight goats.
     Woman: Sorry?
     Girl: Mr Gray's got eight goats.
     Woman: Wow!

Unit 5 Activity G

15

What's the monster playing?

Boy:	I'm reading about a funny monster. It loves sport.
Woman:	Is it playing football?
Boy:	No. It's playing hockey.
Woman:	Does it like playing tennis, too?
Boy:	Not in this story.

What's in the monster's bag?

Boy:	It's got a school bag. It loves school!
Woman:	Great! Are there some crayons in its school bag?
Boy:	No, Mum.
Woman:	Is there some paper to write on?
Boy:	No, Mum. But its tablet is there.

Unit 8 Activity H

25

1 What is Alex doing now?

Woman:	What are you doing now, Alex? Are you playing ball?
Alex:	No. It's the end of our game now.
Woman:	Are you having a drink, then?
Alex:	No, I'm reading about basketball, Grandma!

2 Which sport can Kim do at school?

Man:	Which sport can you do at school, Kim? Badminton?
Kim:	No, but we can do soccer.
Man:	Great! And skateboarding?
Kim:	No, Grandpa! We can't do that!

3 Which ball is in Dad's bag?

Pat:	Have you got a basketball in your bag, Dad?
Dad:	No. I've got a tennis ball, Pat.
Pat:	Fantastic. Have you got a baseball, too?
Dad:	No, I haven't. Sorry.

4 Who is Anna swimming with today?

Boy:	Is Anna swimming with her brother today?
Mum:	That's right. Her friend, Lucy, doesn't like swimming.
Boy:	Oh! Is her grandmother swimming with them, too?
Mum:	Not today.

Song lyrics

Unit 2

Jellyfish! Look, jellyfish!
And sandfish, happy sandfish
Swim, swim, swim
                 in the sea!

Goatfish! Look, goatfish!
And cowfish, funny cowfish
Live in the water,
                 not in a tree!

Catfish! Look, catfish!
And dogfish, scary dogfish!
Swim, swim, swim
                 in the sea!

Sunfish! Look, sunfish!
And starfish, little starfish
Love being in the water,
                 like you and me!

Unit 6

Can you fly a ship?
Don't be silly! No!
Can you fly your kite?

Yes! Yes!

Can you ride on a car?
Don't be silly! No! No!
Can you ride on your sister's motorbike?

Yes! Yes!

Can you drive a bus?
Don't be silly! No!
Can you sit in your dad's truck?

Yes! Yes!

Can you stand on a bike?
Don't be silly! No! No!
Can you stand on your skateboard?

Yes! Yes!

Unit 7

Sing a happy song! Be happy! Be happy!
Now clap your hands. Be happy! Be happy!
Jump and smile and sing my song!
We have a happy song to sing!
Be happy! Be happy!

List of flashcards

These flashcards comprise the Cambridge English: Starters test vocabulary list. The unit references listed here are for Storyfun 2. Flashcards can be found on Presentation plus.

1. bear
2. bee (U2, U3)
3. bird (U2)
4. cat
5. chicken (U2, U4)
6. cow (U2, U4)
7. crocodile (U2)
8. dog
9. donkey
10. duck (U4)
11. elephant
12. fish (U2)
13. frog (U2)
14. giraffe (U2)
15. goat (U4)
16. hippo (U2)
17. horse (U2)
18. jellyfish (U2)
19. lizard (U2)
20. monkey (U2)
21. mouse (U6)
22. pet
23. polar bear (U2)
24. sheep (U4)
25. snake
26. spider (U2)
27. tiger (U2)
28. zebra (U2)
29. arm
30. ears
31. eyes
32. face
33. foot
34. feet
35. hair
36. hand
37. head
38. leg
39. mouth
40. nose
41. smile
42. bag
43. baseball cap (U7)
44. boots (U7)
45. dress
46. glasses (U7)
47. handbag
48. hat
49. jacket (U7)
50. jeans
51. shirt
52. shoes
53. shorts
54. skirt
55. socks
56. trousers
57. T-shirt (U7)
58. watch
59. black
60. blue
61. brown
62. green
63. grey
64. orange
65. pink
66. purple
67. red
68. white
69. yellow
70. baby

71.	boy	113.	water (U2)
72.	brother (U6)	114.	watermelon
73.	dad/father (U6)	115.	armchair (U1)
74.	girl	116.	bath (U1)
75.	grandfather/grandpa	117.	bathroom (U1)
76.	grandmother/grandma	118.	bed (U1)
77.	mum/mother	119.	bedroom (U1)
78.	sister	120.	box
79.	apple (U2)	121.	camera (U3)
80.	banana (U7)	122.	chair (U1)
81.	beans (U4)	123.	clock (U1)
82.	bread	124.	computer (U1)
83.	burger (U7)	125.	cupboard (U1)
84.	cake	126.	desk (U1)
85.	carrot	127.	dining room (U1)
86.	chicken	128.	door (U1)
87.	chips/fries (U1)	129.	flowers
88.	chocolate	130.	garden
89.	coconut (U7)	131.	hall (U1)
90.	egg (U7)	132.	house
91.	fish	133.	kitchen (U1)
92.	grapes (U7)	134.	lamp (U1)
93.	ice cream	135.	living room (U1)
94.	juice (U7)	136.	mat
95.	kiwi (U7)	137.	mirror
96.	lemon	138.	phone
97.	lemonade (U7)	139.	picture
98.	lime (U7)	140.	radio
99.	mango (U7)	141.	rug (U1)
100.	meatballs	142.	sofa
101.	milk (U7)	143.	table (U1)
102.	onion (U4)	144.	television/TV (U1, U3)
103.	orange (U2)	145.	tree
104.	peas (U4)	146.	wall (U1)
105.	pear (U4, U7)	147.	window (U1)
106.	pie (U1)	148.	park
107.	pineapple (U7)	149.	playground
108.	potato (U4)	150.	shop (US store) (U6)
109.	rice (U7)	151.	street (U6)
110.	sausage	152.	zoo
111.	sweets (U1)	153.	board
112.	tomato (U7)	154.	book

155. bookcase (U1)
156. crayons
157. cross
158. eraser (UK rubber)
159. floor (U1)
160. keyboard (computer)
161. mouse (computer) (U6)
162. painting
163. paper
164. pen
165. pencil
166. poster
167. ruler
168. school
169. teacher
170. tick
171. badminton (U8)
172. baseball (U8)
173. basketball (U8)
174. bat (as sports equipment)
175. beach
176. bike (U3, U7)
177. bounce (U8)
178. catch (U8)
179. draw(ing)
180. fishing (U3)
181. football (US soccer) (U5, U8)
182. guitar (U3, U7)
183. hockey (U8)
184. jump (U8)
185. kick (v)
186. kite (U2, U6)
187. piano
188. read
189. run (U8)
190. sing
191. skateboard (U6)
192. skateboarding (U8)
193. swim (v) (U8)
194. table tennis (U8)
195. tennis (U8)
196. tennis racket

197. throw (U8)
198. walk (U8)
199. birthday (party)
200. morning
201. night
202. alien
203. ball
204. balloon
205. board game
206. computer game (U6)
207. doll
208. monster
209. robot
210. teddy bear
211. boat (U2, U6)
212. bus (U6)
213. car (U6)
214. helicopter (U6)
215. lorry (US truck) (U6)
216. motorbike (U6)
217. plane (U6)
218. ship (U6)
219. train (U6)
220. sand (U7)
221. sea
222. shell (U2, U3)
223. sun

Audio track listing

01   Title and copyright

02   Our funny home

03   Our funny home E

04   Our funny home G

05   Jill's jellyfish

06   Jill's jellyfish H

07   Uncle Fred and me

08   Uncle Fred and me E

09   Uncle Fred and me H

10   Mrs Day's garden

11   Mrs Day's garden E

12   Mrs Day's garden H

13   Classmates

14   Classmates C

15   Classmates G

16   I want that game!

17   I want that game! F

18   I want that game! I

19   Monkey beach

20   Monkey beach C

21   Monkey beach E

22   Monkey beach G

23   Winners!

24   Winners! F

25   Winners! H

26   Let's say!

27   Jellyfish song karaoke

28   Can you fly a ship? song karaoke

29   Sing a happy song! karaoke

Acknowledgements

The author would like to acknowledge the shared professionalism and FUN she's experienced whilst working with colleagues during 20 years of production of YLE tests. She would also like to thank CUP for their support in the writing of this second edition of Storyfun.

On a personal note, Karen fondly thanks her inspirational story-telling grandfather, and now, three generations later, her sons, Tom and Will, for adding so much creative fun to our continuation of the family story-telling and story-making tradition.

The author and publishers would like to thank the following ELT professionals who commented on the material at different stages of development: Louise Manicolo, Mexico; Mandy Watkins, Greece.

Design and typeset by Wild Apple Design.

Cover design and header artwork by Nicholas Jackson (Astound).

Sound recordings by Hart McLeod, Cambridge.

Music by Mark Fishlock and produced by Ian Harker. Recorded at The Soundhouse Studios, London.

The authors and publishers acknowledge the following sources of copyright material and are grateful for the permissions granted. While every effort has been made, it has not always been possible to identify the sources of all the material used, or to trace all copyright holders. If any omissions are brought to our notice, we will be happy to include the appropriate acknowledgements on reprinting.

The authors and publishers are grateful to the following illustrators:

Key: B = Bottom; BC = Bottom Centre; BL = Bottom Left; BR = Bottom right; TC = Top Centre; TL = Top Left; TR = Top Right.

David Banks p. 55 (TR)
Isobel Escalante pp. 51, 54 (BC (second from left))
Clive Goodyear pp. 48, 49, 53
Nicholas Jackson p. 5
Kelly Kennedy (Sylvie Poggio) pp. 50, 52, 54 (BL)
Javier Montiel pp. 54 (BC (Second from right))
Gaby Murphy (Advocate) pp. 54 (TL, TR)
Pip Sampson (Graham-Cameron Illustration) pp. 54 (TC, TL (goat))
Melanie Sharp (Sylvie Poggio) pp. 54 (BR)
Alek Sotrirovski (Beehive) p. 46
Chris Sunders p. 5 (TL)

DID YOU KNOW CAMBRIDGE ENGLISH: YOUNG LEARNERS (YLE) IS UPDATING IN 2018?

VISIT **WORLD OF FUN** ONLINE FOR:

| Information about the 2018 test changes | Tips and resources for teaching Young Learners | Official materials to prepare for the updated tests |

www.cambridge.org/worldoffun